Highlights of the Book of Revelation

Highlights of the Book of Revelation

George R. Beasley-Murray

BROADMAN PRESS
Nashville, Tennessee

© Copyright 1972 · Broadman Press
All rights reserved
4213–36
ISBN: 0–8054–1336–7

Library of Congress Catalog Card Number: 70–189501
Dewey Decimal Classification Number: 228
Printed in the United States of America

Preface

This book is an expanded version of lectures on the book of Revelation delivered at the Nationwide Bible Conference, organized by the Sunday School Board of the Southern Baptist Convention and held at Dallas, Texas, March 15–18, 1971. The subject of the conference was "Christian Hope in a Time of Crisis." I had been invited to give a series of biblical expositions on the theme of Christian hope, with special reference to the book of Revelation. In carrying out this task I concentrated on the message contained in the central and closing chapters of that book, believing that most members of the conference would be familiar with its early chapters. In responding to the many requests to have the expositions published, I have rearranged some of the material and added a chapter which deals with the early part of the book of Revelation, so providing an exposition of the whole work.

It will be appreciated that in so short a book as this—and I have deliberately refrained from expanding it—brevity has had to be exercised in the exposition and many issues raised by the book of Revelation ignored. It seemed better to provide a short book which many may read rather than a long one which makes more demands on time and patience than many can give.

When the lectures were delivered, the material was constantly interspersed with readings from the book of Revelation, that the hearers might be reminded of what we were studying. The reader of these pages is urged constantly to refer to the text of the Scripture—even to read whole chapters when necessary—so that the cogency or otherwise of the expositions might rightly be judged. The chief intention of this little book is to help the reader gain a better understanding of the book of Revelation. The usefulness of these pages will be in proportion to the extent that they drive the reader to study the book itself.

I record my deepest gratitude to the Sunday School Board for the privilege of ministering to the conference, and in particular to Dr. A. V. Washburn, the presiding officer of the conference, who corresponded with me frequently about the lectures and encouraged me to prepare them for publication. My one regret in sending out the book to a wider readership is that it cannot convey the lively discussion which the lectures provoked from a distinguished panel of speakers. Dr. Herschel Hobbs, its chairman, Dr. Theodore Adams, Dr. Kenneth Chafin, Dr. Duke McCall and Dr. T. A. Patterson dealt with a speaker from foreign parts with greatest charity and delighted as well as instructed the assembled conference members with their reflections on the material. They undoubtedly added the relish and the sauce to the dishes I provided. If this book can stimulate discussion of the order that took place in the conference, it will well serve its purpose.

Contents

1. **An Introduction to the Book of Revelation** — 1

2. **The Aim of Hope: Faithful Obedience to the Limit** — 10
   Chapters 1—3

3. **The Endurance of Hope: The Church in Conflict** — 26
   Chapters 4—5, 10—14

4. **The Dark Side of Hope: The Judgment of the Nations** — 45
   Chapters 6—9, 15—19

5. **The Goal of Hope: The Coming of Christ and His Kingdom** — 64
   Chapters 19:11 to 22:21

Chapter 1
An Introduction to the Book of Revelation

The book of Revelation gained its name from the very first Greek word in the book, *apokalupsis,* revelation. A "revelation" is an uncovering of what is hidden or the removal of a veil to show what lies behind it. This book therefore sets out to open the curtains of history and enable us to see what happens to man and how the human story ends. It is as though we were brought into a theater in which a cycle of historical plays is being performed; when the curtain falls on this one, we are presented with a succession of scenes in which the unfolding drama of history reaches its climax.

This presentation, however, has no ordinary dramatist for its author. The real title of the book is not, as the honored King James Version has it, "The Revelation of St. John the Divine," but "The Revelation of *Jesus Christ,* which *God* gave him . . . and he made it known to his servant John" (v. 1). When we go on to examine the book, we find that its central figure is Jesus Christ himself, and the dominating theme of the story is the victory of God the Almighty over all who seek to frustrate his purpose. I am reminded of an oratorio which I saw and heard performed during a Christian congress in Hamburg, Germany. The oratorio was presented by the composer, who also conducted the orchestra and sang the leading part—he had a busy time that night! So it is with this book: It is none other than God who pulls the curtain apart to enable us to see the events depicted. The plot is his creation, he directs the drama, and he is the leading figure of the production. It is his will that is performed, and not in the last act only.

In many respects this book of Revelation is unique. In its form, however, it is not. We now know that in the period when it was written a considerable number of works written in a similar style appeared on the market. So far as I am aware John's book was the first actually to call itself a "revelation," but because it is the supreme instance of this type of writing it gave its name to all others like it. They are called "revelations," or rather, since the word for revelation in the language in which John's book was originally written (Greek) is *apokalupsis*, they are commonly known as "apocalypses." The earliest example of this sort of publication is the book of Daniel in the Old Testament. It set the fashion for a considerable number of imitators, though of course they were never included in the Bible. They circulated chiefly in the last two centuries B.C. and in the first two centuries of the Christian era. Most of them bear the name of a saint of ancient times, in whose name they were written. So we find more than one book ascribed to Enoch, an Apocalypse of Abraham, the Testaments of the Twelve Patriarchs (claiming to give the last words of the twelve sons of Jacob), the Assumption of Moses, the Apocalypse of Baruch (the scribe of Jeremiah), a work purporting to come from Ezra the scribe (the so-called 2 Esdras in the Apocrypha), and so on. Most of these works became lost in the course of the centuries, but one by one they have come to light during the past hundred years, and they have been very closely studied. Their chief value is the light they throw on the language and picture symbolism of Daniel, Revelation, and related passages in other books of the Bible.

The authors of these books tried to follow in the steps of the Old Testament prophets. They did their best to keep alive the faith of the prophets in times when the flame of faith and hope burned low. Not infrequently they were motivated in their writing by the activities of tyrants who oppressed the people of God, and so they tried to convey messages of hope for God's saints in dark days. Above all, they looked for the fulfilment of God's promise of a kingdom in which sin and death and sorrow would be swallowed up. Large tracts of apocalyptic writings are written in the style of the old prophets, but especially characteristic of them are descriptions of visions received in trance or dream. Many of these visions take the form of highly colored parables, in which angels and demons abound and people and nations are depicted in the guise of animals.

Here is a typical account of a vision, taken from the Testament of the Twelve Patriarchs:

Hear the vision which I saw. I saw twelve harts feeding. And nine of them were dispersed. Now the three were preserved, but on the following day they also were dispersed.

And I saw that the three harts became three lambs, and they cried to the Lord, and he brought them forth into a flourishing and well watered place, yea he brought them out of darkness into light. And there they cried unto the Lord until there gathered unto them the nine harts, and they became as twelve sheep, and after a little time they increased and became many flocks. . . . And I saw . . . a lamb, and on his right was as it were a lion; and all the beasts and all the reptiles rushed against him, and the lamb overcame them and destroyed them.

I have omitted some complicating features of the vision, but the meaning of its essential features can, I think, be guessed by most readers of the Old Testament. The twelve harts are clearly the twelve tribes of Israel. They were taken into captivity at two different periods, but at length they were restored to their land, first as a small company and then joined by the rest. The harts became "lambs," i.e., they became the true flock of God. Out of the midst of the flock a leader arises as their champion, a younger member of God's flock (a "lamb of God"), and he fights their enemies and destroys them. The vision goes on to show that the time of troubles then comes to its end and gives place to the prosperity of the kingdom of God. It is worth noting that although a lion stands at the right of the lamb, it is the lamb and not the lion who fights and overcomes the beasts. This reflects a belief that God will raise up two messiahs, not one. The messiah from the priestly tribe of Levi will appear with the messiah from the tribe of Judah, and the priest-messiah will take precedence over the king-messiah. This was the view, apparently, of the Qumran community.

It will be appreciated that people accustomed to reading books and hearing sermons that used this kind of symbolism would find little difficulty in getting the message from them. The closest modern parallel to such a method of communication is the political cartoon, which is a fairly standard feature in the daily press of most countries. The purpose of cartoons is the embodiment of a message relating to the concrete situations of the day—indeed they reflect judgments on the doings and the fluctuating fortunes both of national and of international groups and alliances. Significantly, from our point of view, cartoonists often employ stereotyped symbols of men and of animals, to represent parties and nations, and frequently they set their characters in bizarre and exaggerated situations in order to convey their messages the more plainly. So it was with the apocalyptists when they recounted their visions.

The *Reader's Digest* often quotes cartoon headings for our amusement. It occurred to me that we could construct a few of our own with a more serious intent which a cartoonist could take and illustrate with appropriate pictures. Consider for example the following sentence: "Uncle Sam and John Bull ought to shake hands; they can't afford another Boston Tea Party." That sentiment contains a message which a cartoonist could depict with the greatest ease. Here is another, which employs established animal symbols: "The American Eagle and the British Lion should woo the Russian bear, for the Chinese Dragon is breathing fire over the nations." A cartoonist could put a bit of amusement into his illustration of that one, and he could make it thoroughly contemporary by giving the beasts suitable faces, e.g., the eagle a resemblance to Nixon, the lion a nose like Ted Heath's, the bear Kosygin's features, and the dragon the round face of Mao. It so happens that I concocted that for the lectures embodied in this book in March, 1971. Shortly afterwards the extraordinary episode took place in China of the table tennis matches between American and Chinese teams; it gave the cartoonists of the world a marvelous opportunity to have fun at the expense of Nixon and Mao and a few other aspirants after political Ping-Pong!

Now the ancient apocalyptists did something very much like this in their own day but with the utmost seriousness of purpose. Many of the symbols which they used in portraying the political powers of their times —as well as the spiritual powers which they saw behind them—were as traditional as Uncle Sam, John Bull, the Russian Bear, and the Chinese Dragon. For example, the many headed, many horned dragon of the book of Revelation, who in chapter 13 is said to emerge from the sea, is none other than the sea monster of primitive Middle East religious traditions. In an ancient saga, which circulated throughout the lands of the nearer Orient, the sea monster was an evil spiritual power that defied the powers of heaven, but finally it was defeated and rendered impotent. (In one form of the story the monster's body became the stuff out of which the universe was made.) In due time the monster became the standing symbol for evil political powers (see, e.g., Isa. 27:1; 51:9–10; Dan. 7:21 ff). By the application of the figure to oppressor nations, both the nature of their governments was indicated and their sure fate through the judgment of God. In the book of Revelation this symbolism is applied alike to the antichristian empire, and to its ruler. Above all it is applied to the devil who stands behind all the evil works of the world.

The crucial thing about the book of Revelation, of course, is not its pictures—its cartoons, if you like—but the message which is conveyed through them. This message is fundamentally the same as that which is contained in the teaching of Jesus in the Gospels and of the apostles in Acts and the Epistles, relating to the redemption and the victory of our Lord. The message is developed and applied to the world of the author's day, and from that setting the issues and the end of history are portrayed.

Such an application was needed because the church of that time was a church under the cross—a "cross" which was being provided by the same world power that set up the cross of Jesus. The struggle of the church is depicted by John in the light of the conflict of the ages. He labors to show that the contest was actually settled by the cross and resurrection of Jesus, and that it is to be brought to a glorious conclusion at the coming of Jesus. To a church under the cross there is revealed the victory of the cross and the glory that must follow.

At this point, before we embark on a review of the teaching of the book of Revelation, it may be helpful to suggest an outline of its contents.

The book opens with a vision of the risen Christ. This may be compared with the vision which Isaiah had in the Temple courts (Isa. 6) or that which Ezekiel received by the river Chebar (Ezek. 1). Just as those prophets were called in the visions of God which they saw, so John was called by Christ to prophesy in his name. And just as the visions given to those two prophets to no small degree conditioned their presentation of the message they had to proclaim, so John's vision of Christ sets the tone for all he is given to see and declare. The Christ is revealed as the risen Lord who holds the keys of death (1:18), and as the sovereign Lord of the universe he holds the churches in his right hand (1:20); in that almighty hand the churches are secure, no matter how furiously the antichrist may rage.

The vision of the risen Lord leads to messages to the churches which he holds in his hand (chaps. 2—3). In a similar way the vision of God and the Redeemer, described in chapters 4—5, leads directly to the visions of the end which immediately follow. The lengthy series of judgments on the rebellious world, described in chapters 6—19, flow out of that central vision. These judgments are portrayed under three series of symbols: those which result from the opening of seven seals of the book of destiny (6:1 to 8:5), those which are heralded by the sounding of seven trumpets (8:6 to 11:19), and those which follow from the pouring out of seven bowls or cups of wrath (15—16). As I hope to show later, when we consider these chapters in detail, it would seem that the visions do not unfold successive series of catastrophes that follow one another in chronological order, rather they describe in a threefold way under different images the judgments of the last times. Accordingly each of these three series concludes with a glimpse of the coming of the kingdom of God; that is, each series brings us to the end of this age (see 8:1 ff; 11:15; 16:17).

Between the second and third series of judgments there is a pause in the movement of the story, that the reader may grasp how the church fares in this period of the divine judgments. The "pause" is made up of two series of short prophecies, narrated in chapters 10—11 and chapters 12—14. These passages are of great importance, for they enable us to grasp the significance of the events which are described in the book as a whole.

The account of the judgments is followed by a representation of the coming of Christ in chapter 19, and then of the glories of the final kingdom of God (20—22). A short epilogue concludes the work (22:6–21).

Chapter 2
The Aim of Hope: Faithful Obedience to the Limit
Revelation 1—3

I. Prologue: Revelation 1:1-8

The introduction to John's book states its origin and includes a greeting from the author to his readers in the style that was customary in his time. Short as they are, these opening two paragraphs contain some deeply significant utterances. Just as the prologue to the Gospel of John puts the reader in a position to understand the story of Jesus that follows, so the prologue to the Revelation of John supplies a context from which the reader may understand the vision of history that follows.

The "revelation" at the heart of this book is the gift of God to Jesus Christ (v. 1). It is sent by the mediation of an angel to John, who in turn writes it down for the seven churches in the Roman province of Asia, and so it is imparted to the whole church. Because it has such an origin, the content of the book can be described as "the word of God" and "the testimony of Jesus Christ" (v. 2); i.e., it proclaims God's message and the witness borne by Jesus Christ. Accordingly a blessing is pronounced on the man who reads the prophecy to an assembled congregation of God's people, as also to

Faithful Obedience to the Limit

those in the congregation who listen to it (v. 3). It is assumed that both reader and hearer "heed what is written in it" (v. 3).

The greeting voiced by John to the seven churches invokes a blessing from God the Father, Son, and Spirit (vv. 4–5), but the terms in which he does it are unique and extraordinarily significant.

First, God is described as he "who is and who was and who is to come." The title almost certainly echoes the name of God revealed to Moses at the burning bush (Ex. 3:14 f). In the translation of the Old Testament into Greek, which was read by most of the early Christians, the name of God is rendered in this passage, "I am he who is." That name has been expanded by John to include the past and the future. God is Lord of the ages that have gone, of the present, and of the ages that are to come. But instead of completing the name by the phrase "and who is to *be,*" John writes "and who is to *come.*" God is not merely the one who exists in all future ages, but he who is to come and perform his mighty acts to achieve his eternal purpose. It is of the nature of God that he "comes" to work his gracious and all-powerful will.

Instead of the Spirit, John speaks of "the seven spirits before his throne." Why seven, and not one? Scholars are able to adduce archaeological reasons to explain the origin of the seven spirits, and I fancy that their learned digging into the past would have made John's eyes blink in surprise. He himself would have given a simple explanation: "Why seven, and not one? He is the Spirit whom the Lord sends to his congregations with fulness of blessing. I was commissioned to write to the *seven* churches, who symbolize the whole church (see 2:7). So my greeting comes from the Spirit, who proceeds from the throne of God in his fulness to minister to the church of God in its completeness."

Jesus Christ is described as "the faithful witness, the firstborn from the dead and ruler of the kings of the earth." This book embodies the "witness" that the risen Christ has borne. Naturally his witness is at all times "faithful," and can be trusted. First-century Christians, however, remembered that Jesus was a faithful witness in the days of his flesh and that he fearlessly bore his testimony when he was on trial for his life. This was an inspiration to the members of the early church, as they faced the prospect of being brought to trial for the sake of the name and the gospel of Christ (see 1 Tim. 6:13). The readers of this book, faced with the prospect of appalling tests of faith, are reminded that Jesus kept the faith, even to the end.

This faithful witness is "the firstborn from the dead." He was put to death for his testimony, but he was raised by God to be the first among a multitude of the children of God, who one day will rise to share his glorious likeness and his triumphant kingdom. The Jew was familiar with the fact that the firstborn took first place in a family; so too as the "firstborn of the dead," the risen Christ is Lord of the *dead.* But he is also Lord of the *living!* (See Rom. 14:9.) Yet further, he is "ruler of the kings of earth." The emperors of Rome regarded themselves as supreme among the kings of earth. They used their power to oppose the church of Christ, and John looks to the time when they will give place to an antichrist, who will use every artifice of earth and hell to crush the church out of existence. The risen Jesus however is Lord not only of the Caesars but of antichrist himself. Let the church of Christ then take heart: their Savior has all authority in heaven and on earth and over hell!

Accordingly, a doxology of grateful love to the glory of Christ is sung (vv. 5–6), and a declaration made of the sure promise of his coming, when every eye shall see him (v. 7).

In affirmation of the unassailable certainty of the triumph of God in the reigning and returning Christ, John adds the declaration of the Father: "I am Alpha and Omega" (v. 8). Most Christians, whatever their language, are aware that alpha and omega are the first and last letters of the alphabet used by the Greeks. Alpha is the name given to the letter *a*, and omega is the name for the long *o* (sounded as in "wrote"). For God to affirm that he is *"A* and *O"* is as though he were to say, "I am *A* and *Z."* That implies, "I am the beginning and the end of the alphabet of all life." We know that the Jews used this way of speaking to represent not alone the beginning and the end of something but the whole process between. It was said by the rabbis that Adam transgressed the law from *A* to *Z*, and that, by contrast, Abraham kept the law from *A* to *Z*. Accordingly, for God to state that he is *A* and *Z* implies that he is the Lord of all history—Lord of its beginning, Lord of its end, and Lord of all that lies between. We recall that the same affirmation is made by the Christ in Revelation 22:13. This implies a conviction which underlies this entire book from its first page to its last: God performs his works of mercy and judgment and exercises his reign through his Son, the Lord Jesus Christ.

II. The Vision of Christ: Revelation 1:9–20

John received his vision of the risen Christ on "the Lord's day" (1:10). This is the earliest appearance in Christian literature of the term "the Lord's day" for Sunday, and a very meaningful term it must have been for Christians in the Roman world. There is evidence to show that in some parts of the empire, notably in Egypt and in Asia Minor, "Emperor's Day" was observed every month, and in some areas it was even a day of the week, in honor of the emperor's accession to his throne. Some unknown group of Christians must have taken the cue from this custom and said, "There's one day above all others which deserves to be celebrated, and that is the day on which our Savior rose from the dead to be sovereign Lord of universe. Sunday is *our Lord's day.*" And so it came to be through all the church. It's a good name. It deserves to be perpetuated, and the day itself used for Christ's royal service.

The terms in which the risen Lord is described are drawn from the picture of the Son of man in Daniel 7:13, as also of a glorious heavenly being in Daniel 10: 5 f, and of God himself in Daniel 7:9. The Christ combines in himself the splendor of the saints of God, of the angels of heaven, and of the eternal God.

Consonant with this vision of glory, Christ declares himself to be "the first and the last and the living one" (v. 17); that is, *he* is Alpha and Omega, the beginning and the end, and the living Lord of all that lies between. As such, he has the key of death and of "hades," the realm of the dead (v. 18). Since he is the Lord of death,

Faithful Obedience to the Limit

he has power to open the gates that close on the dead and to raise the dead to eternal life in God's glorious kingdom. His followers, who may soon be threatened by death from the enemies of the Christ, must never allow this truth to fall from their vision.

The first thing that John hears is a voice commanding him to write to the seven churches that which he now sees and is to see. The first thing on which his gaze rests—even before his eyes light on Christ—is seven lamps, which represent the churches. The Christ is seen in the midst of his people—their life, their inspiration, and their protector. The picture comes from the vision in Zechariah 4, where a single golden lampstand represents Israel, separated for the service of God in the world. The fact that John sees seven lamps, and not simply one, indicates that it is in the local churches that *the* church is to be seen, and these cannot be understood apart from the Christ in their midst.

As to the seven churches, it is well known that they were grouped around Ephesus, the greatest center of population in Asia Minor. It is likely that each of the seven churches was itself the center of lesser groups of churches. Since the churches in Asia Minor were becoming increasingly important in the period of John's writing, to address these seven was a fitting mode of addressing the whole church of Christ at that time.

The vision depicts the churches not only as lamps among which Christ walks, but as stars in his hand (v. 16). These stars are said to be the "angels of the seven churches" (v. 20). This is a puzzling statement. If that means that the stars represent the guarding angels of the churches, it seems a strange procedure for the risen

Lord to send messages to them by means of the prophet John (the letters are addressed in each case to the angel of the church, see 2:1). Nor is it likely, as was formerly maintained, that the angels of the churches are the ministers of the churches, however fitting a description of ministers that may be held by ministers-to-be! A clue to John's meaning may be gained in the observation that while the angel of the church is addressed in each of the letters, the members of the church are actually in view in all that is said in them. Accordingly, the angels of the churches most probably signify the churches themselves viewed as in Christ, and so in heaven, in distinction from the existence which they have to maintain in the world, in the midst of the dirt and temptations and trials which characterize life on earth.

The symbolism of the churches as "angels" would have been more easily understood in the first-century Orient than it is among twentieth-century men in the West, but the reality implied in the symbolism is right up-to-date. For the church is still characterized by imperfections in its concrete life in the world, but mercifully its relation to the holy risen Christ is more important still. For that which makes the church the church is not the frailty of its members but the presence of Christ in its midst.

It is not difficult to see why this imagery is employed at this point in John's book. In the letters which follow, the imperfections and sins of the churches have the blazing searchlight of Christ's gaze focused upon them. "Repent" is the most prominent command in the messages of the risen Lord. Hardly a reference is made to the sins of the world, except insofar as the church is guilty of them. These churches are composed of men and women of very frail flesh. How can they possibly survive in the onslaughts of the world under antichrist? Yet before a word of rebuke is uttered by the Lord of the churches, they are reminded that they are in the right hand of him who is the Lord of the universe.

This is underscored by the symbolism of the seven stars in Christ's right hand. For the seven stars were originally the seven planets, which pagans regarded as rulers of the world. The picture of the seven planets was appropriated by the Romans as a sign of the universal political power of the Caesars, and it often appeared on Roman coins in this sense. John's use of the picture here is akin to his use of the term "Lord's day" for Sunday: as Jesus rose to be Lord of the universe on his Easter, and Christians celebrate this every Sunday, so the sovereignty over this world is destined to be given to the despised churches, which are in the right hand of the Lord of heaven and earth.

When therefore the weaknesses of the church are exposed in the letters addressed to the churches, their heavenly existence in Christ is not for a moment denied, least of all by John. If he writes in scathing terms about the churches in the seven letters, he adopts a very different tone in the rest of the book; for in the visions that follow he consistently raises our eyes to look on the church in its heavenly aspect, as it is maintained by the right hand of Christ. The church may be the object of the wrath of the evil powers of this world and of all that belong to them, but it exists in the care of God and of his Christ, and it is destined to rule in the kingdom which will succeed the kingdoms of this world.

The keynote of the letters, therefore, is that of the responsibility laid on the people of God to be true and faithful representatives of Christ in the world. This is why sharp words are used which never occur later. The Christ who loves his church reproves it, that it may fulfil its task in the world now and attain its destiny in the day of his glory.

III. The Letters to the Churches: Revelation 2—3

These chapters are the best known, most commented on, and most frequently preached on in the book of Revelation. I shall therefore deal with them very briefly in these groupings.

1. Letters to Churches Troubled by False Teachers

The activity of men who claim apostolic authority for a nonapostolic message is referred to at the beginning of the letter to **Ephesus** (2:2). In the letter to **Pergamum** they are said to hold the teaching of Balaam and of the Nicolaitans (2:14–15). In the letter to **Thyatira** doctrines of this kind are upheld by a prophetess whom John labels Jezebel (2:20); among other things she teaches "what they like to call the deep secrets of Satan" (2:24). These men and women must have been similar to those who are denounced in the second letter of Peter and in the letter of Jude. History knows them as Gnostics, the "Knowers," for they proclaimed a special kind of knowledge ("gnosis" is the Greek word for knowledge) as the only way of salvation. It was a fundamental tenet of these people that matter is evil, and therefore everything belonging to the creation is evil. This led some Gnostics to become ascetic and to renounce life in this world, including marriage. It led others to believe that since only the spiritual is good and the material worthless, it was irrelevant what you did in and with the body, and they indulged in all kinds of excesses, including gross immorality. It will be readily appreciated that when people with these views gained access to the churches they had devastating effects on less perceptive Christians. In particular they despised the so-called "apostolic decrees" (Acts 15:28–29), which were formulated at the Council of Jerusalem as a means of enabling Jewish and Gentile believers to associate together in one fellowship. From every point of view, therefore, these teachers were a threat to the existence of the church and had to be opposed. Their activity in the churches of Asia Minor is clearly reflected in 2:14 f; 2:20–24.

The church at Ephesus is commended for rejecting the preachers of false doctrine (2:2). But its members had one fault: "You have lost your early love" (2:4). We tend to think that this must refer primarily to a cooling of a love to Christ, but in view of what immediately follows ("Repent, and do as you once did"), it is more likely that love to people, shown in loving affection, is especially in mind. In reality, of course, love to our fellows in God's way cannot exist without love to God, nor can love to God without love for people (Matt. 12:30 f, 1 John 4:20). So the call is sounded, "Repent!" For lovelessness kills a church.

Pergamum is named as the place "where Satan has his throne" (2:13). This relates to a great altar to Zeus, standing on a platform cut out of rock on a hill that was covered with temples and which dominated the city. Here also the church is called on to repent, for the followers of Balaam are a greater threat to a church than persecutors ever can be.

Thyatira was a city full of trade guilds, each of which owned allegiance to a patron deity. The Christians here are commanded to make no compromise with evil. They are bidden to hold on to the apostolic decree (2:24), and to hold fast in obedient faith until the Lord comes (2:25).

To believers who persist in the Christian way, and so overcome the obstacles put in the way of Christian discipleship, promises are given of participating in the fruit of the tree of life (2:7); of eating the hidden manna of the kingdom of God; of being given a white stone with a secret name (2:18, perhaps a revelation of Christ's name and a guarantee of his protecting care to the end); and a share in the sovereignty of the kingdom of Christ (2:26 ff).

2. Letters to Churches Troubled by Persecutors

The churches of **Smyrna** and **Philadelphia** receive no blame in the messages sent to them, only sympathy and encouragement from Christ.

The Smyrna church is opposed by the Jews who live in that city (2:9). Here is anti-Semitism in reverse—a not uncommon phenomenon in the early years of the church's existence. Justin Martyr, who lived in the mid-second century, reported that Jews cursed in their synagogues those who believed in Jesus the Messiah. Tertullian, at the end of that century, told how Jews sometimes instigated persecutions of Christians.

It so happens that a letter from the church of Smyrna, written in the second century A.D., has been preserved to us. It recounts in some detail the martyrdom of their leader Polycarp, and describes how the Jews in Smyrna joined the pagans in accusing Polycarp of hostility to the State religion—an extraordinary accusation for Jews to make. "This is the teacher of Asia," they cried, "the father of the Christians, the puller down of our gods, who teaches numbers not to sacrifice nor to worship." They were especially enthusiastic in collecting timber and faggots for the burning of Polycarp, even though it took place on the sabbath day. The Jews of Smyrna in John's day evidently resembled those in the time of Polycarp; in such circumstances John was compelled to represent the "synagogue of the Lord" in Smyrna as the "synagogue of Satan" (2:9), a terrible indictment to have to make.

In his address to Smyrna the Lord speaks of himself as the conqueror of death, who can give the same victory to his followers (2:8). If they are faithful to the end he will give them the "crown of life" (2:10), i.e., the joy and honor of life in the kingdom that is to come.

Jews who oppose the church of Christ appear to be active in Philadelphia also (3:7 ff). The Lord affirms that he is the one who has "the key of David." That is, he possesses the power to open the door of the kingdom to his people. When he opens it, none can shut it against them. But who would claim to be able to shut out believers from the kingdom of God? Probably the Jews of Philadelphia. They may well have taunted Christians that they had no part in God's kingdom, for they were accursed heretics. In reply to such charges the Lord states: "I have set before you an open door, which no one can shut" (3:8). This is not a door of service for Christ, but the door to life, which he alone can open who has David's key. The Christians at Philadelphia belong to the King, and their place in his kingdom is sure. "I will make those of Satan's synagogue . . . come and fall down at your feet; and they shall know that you are my beloved people" (2:9). This seems to be an adaptation of a similar promise in the Old Testament made to faithful Jews (Isa. 49:23; 60:14). Faithless Jews will find their privilege reversed.

The promise is made to the overcomer of Philadelphia that he will become a pillar in God's temple; that is, he will be rooted in God's house. The name of God, of Jerusalem, and of Christ will be on him; so he belongs to them forever.

3. Churches Troubled by Their Spiritual Poverty

The church in **Sardis** shared the character of the city itself: it had a glorious past and a poor present (3:1). The sociologist is inclined to say that this is normal! It may be. But the Lord expects something better of his people than weak conformity to the world in which they are set. Why should churches in depressed areas themselves be depressed? Is the victory of Christ only for affluent suburbanites? "Wake up!" the Lord calls out. "Put some strength into what is left. Remember the teaching you received. Observe it, and repent" (3:3). He who overcomes will walk in white garments (3:4). That is a striking promise to a church in a city with a wool industry! The clothes which Christ gives, however, are garments of glory in the day of resurrection. The alternative to wearing that kind of robe is to be naked and ashamed in the judgment, with no place in the roll of the citizens of the kingdom (3:5).

Laodicea was the wealthiest city in its area. As in Sardis the church in this city took the character of its environment: it was materially rich, but spiritually poor (3:17). The "advice" of verse 18 reflects three features of Laodicea for which it was famous: it possessed banks, a cloth industry, and a medical school with a renowned eye salve. So the men of the banking world are counseled to "buy" real gold, which outlasts this world; the clothiers are to produce clothes for the real man; the medical men are to secure ointment which can cure spiritual blindness and enable them to see the truth of God. How can they get such things? By heeding the words of Christ: "Repent . . . and open the door!" (vv. 19–20). These are remarkable words, for they are addressed not to pagans outside the church, but to people who regarded themselves as Christians but who had given no place to Christ in their lives. Yet more remarkable is the promise that follows the appeal: to the least deserving the most gracious of all promises is spoken, "To him who is victorious I will grant a place on my throne, as I myself was victorious and sat down with my Father on his throne" (v. 21).

All the churches are bidden to receive the message given to Laodicea, even as they should those given to the other churches. For Laodicea's failure is the perpetual threat to the church. Our only safeguard is repentance and total surrender to the Lord who has redeemed us.

Conclusion

Our theme has been the responsibility of the people of God to be the faithful church of the faithful Christ. Set in the world as lamps for Christ, it is called to be the light of the world (Matt. 5:12), even as the Lord is the light of the world (John 8:12). Where it fails of its high calling, appeal is made for it to repent and fulfil its vocation.

It is likely that these lines will be read chiefly by men and women who exercise leadership in the church of Christ. The seven letters were addressed to the churches in their totality. How carefully should they be listened to by those of us who are responsible for the churches themselves! For it is hardly likely that churches will take to themselves messages of this kind if it is apparent that their leaders do not.

Three churches were called on to beware of the laxity of the followers of Balaam. Perhaps none need to beware of this more than ministers, who can easily exempt themselves of high standards in areas where their congregations cannot see them. We recall that Balaam was a preacher, a prophet who misused his extraordinary gift. How do we who preach stand in this respect?

Ephesus had lost its early love. Of how many preachers, Sunday School teachers, theological students, and others of us who labor in the church has this been true? But is any influence more calculated to kill the ministry of the word than such a state?

The church of Sardis had a name for being alive, but it was dead. Has that any relation to my church? More pertinent still: has it any application to me? "Splendid man, so-and-so; sound as a bell, right on the ball spiritually!" So it may be said of me, and how little they guess that I am spiritually feeble, losing my grip on spiritual realities, in danger of being rejected by him who knows my heart (1 Cor. 9:27). Can it be that I am neither hot, nor cold, but lukewarm? In God's sight pitiful, poor, blind, naked? Or on the way to that state?

If I contemptuously dismiss such questions, I need to read the letters again, and then make certain that I have not left the company of Jesus and joined the Pharisees. Sinners saved by grace are more sober.

Dora Greenwell, a contemporary and admirer of Spurgeon, once had a conversation with a woman eighty-four years of age, who had been converted at the age of eighty. Dora repeated the woman's testimony in the following words:

If you ask me how long I have been in the world, I'm old—
    I'm very old;
If you ask me how many years I've lived, it'll very soon be
    told—
Past eighty years of age, yet only four years old!

Spiritual maturity has nothing to do with chronological age. We who are servants of the word know full well that it has also nothing to do with church office.

While we are on pilgrimage we need to recall the great words of the letters of Christ: *Repent! Wake up! Remember! Hold Fast!* With these watchwords in our hearts and a prayer for the grace of obedience on our lips the promises to him who overcomes will surely be ours.

Chapter 3
The Endurance of Hope: The Church in Conflict

Revelation 4—5, 10—14

The chapters of the book of Revelation which we are now to consider depict not so much the movement of its story as the context in which the story is set.

Chapters 4—5 contain a vision of heaven, described in such a way as to enable us to grasp that *the redemption of Christ is the turning point of history.*

Chapters 10—11 have a variety of themes, the chief of which is *the church as the witnessing people of God in the time of conflict.*

Chapters 12—14 teach that *the conflict between the Lamb and the dragon is the clue to history.*

We shall look at these passages in order and consider some of the lessons that they teach us.

(1) The vision of God and the Lamb in chapters 4—5 forms the fulcrum of the book of Revelation. The whole movement of world history is determined by what is here described. Before we are allowed to look at the chaos on earth, we are bidden to fix our gaze on heaven and see who occupies the throne of the universe.

Who is it who sits on the throne? In chapter 4 the sole occupant of the throne is God almighty, the creator of the universe. Every word of John's description is calculated to impress us with the reality of God's glory, holiness, majesty, and power. There is no mention of man in this picture. Celestial beings alone adore the all-holy Creator. In chapter 5 the scene changes. Here the center of attention is the Lamb who was slain but now is risen, and the redeemed children of God join the angels and all creation in paeans of praise to God and the Lamb. The contrast of scenes is deliberate, in order to emphasize the wonder of that which Christ has achieved for man.

Martin Kiddle summarized the thought of these two chapters as follows:

> The general purpose of chapters 4 and 5 is then clear enough. In chapter 4 the theme is that of the omnipotent Creator, reigning majestic and remote in a heaven from which man is excluded. The God whom John sees is the God whom Isaiah and Ezekiel saw. The heaven he sees is the heaven of the old dispensation. In chapter 5 the focus of the seer's eyes changes, and with incomparably dramatic force he describes his vision of the Redeemer in whom lies every hope of man's salvation, every hope of a future kingdom of justice.[1]

The symbolism under which Christ's redeeming work is portrayed is that of the opening of a book which has been sealed but which none could previously open or read. What does this book represent? All are agreed that it must in some sense be a book of destiny, a record of God's judgments and deliverances which must happen in order to bring about his purpose of good for the universe.

The suggestion has been made that the book is, in fact, the "testament" of God. We are indebted to Theodore Zahn for this interpretation. He wrote:

> The word *biblion* itself permits of many interpretations, but for the readers of that time it was designated by the seven seals on its back beyond possibility of a mistake. Just as in Germany before the introduction of money orders everyone knew that a letter sealed with five seals contained money, so the most simple member of the Asiatic churches knew that a biblion made fast with seven seals was a testament. When a testator died the testament was brought forward, and, when possible opened in the presence of seven witnesses who sealed it; i.e., it was unsealed, read aloud, and executed. . . . The document with seven seals is a symbol of the promise of a future kingdom. The disposition long ago occurred and was documented and sealed, but it was not yet carried out.[2]

The symbolism, therefore, conveys the teaching that God's will to bestow upon men a kingdom of grace and glory is carried out by Christ. He has won the right to do this by his death and resurrection. Indeed by this act he has set men free to enter the kingdom. He has "purchased for God men of every tribe and language, people and nation . . . and they shall reign upon earth."

Observe: *the crucial act has happened.* The redemption has taken place, and the Lamb is on the throne. God's rule of grace through the slain and risen Lamb has begun. Soon the Lamb of God will open the seals of God's testament and so initiate the judgments which will culminate in the kingdom of glory. The time between the death and resurrection of Christ and his final appearing is ignored in order to emphasize the fact that the redeeming and judging acts of God, which issue in the kingdom of the new creation, are wrought through the Christ, who holds all ages in his grasp.

Here in the central vision of the book is comfort for the people of God. The purpose of the dying and rising of Jesus was the coming of God's kingdom, and that the people of God might have a place in it. His enthronement signifies that it *has* come and it is the pledge that it *will* come. If the king bears the scars of his sacrifice, it is not surprising that his people should suffer in the present; but as those scars are the ground of their hope for his kingdom, so their sufferings are the prelude to the glory which they will share with him.

(2) The chapters which occupy the middle of John's book (10—14) interrupt the descriptions of the messianic judgments and illuminate the position of the church in this time. We are enabled to see that the struggle in which the Christians of John's day are involved is much more than the resistance of a little group to Caesar worship in a province of the Roman Empire. Their struggle is part of a more terrifying contest, in which the age-old adversary of God strives by every subterfuge of politics and religion to thwart God's purpose in his church. By the method he has adopted, John takes a position similar to that which is observable in chapter 5: the time between the two advents is compressed, and although he is concerned to illuminate the situation of the church in the end time, he actually portrays the role of the church throughout the time between the advents.

The burden of the opening paragraph of chapter 10 is a declaration of the nearness of the end and the coming of the promised kingdom of God when the seventh angel sounds his trumpet. The rendering of verse 6 in the King James Version, that there shall be "time no longer," is misleading. *The New English Bible* makes the meaning clear: "There shall be no more *delay;* but when the time comes for the seventh angel to sound his trumpet, the hidden purpose of God will have been fulfilled, as he promised to his servants the prophets."

John then relates that an angel hands him a scroll to eat (compare Ezek. 2:9 ff). The contents of the scroll are presumably the rest of John's book. John is confirmed in his prophetic commission and commanded to continue his witness. As with Ezekiel, the eating of the book caused both sweetness and bitterness, corresponding to the mixture of blessings and woes in the prophecies. A prophetic ministry cannot avoid this kind of experience. Only the false prophet proclaims the sweet and is silent about the bitter elements of the divine word.

Chapter 11 depicts, in two short prophecies, the position of the people of Christ and their function in the world in the last time. It provides one of the clearest examples of the way in which John, the Christian prophet, utilizes the pictures and traditions of contemporary Jewish prohecy in order to convey his message.

The opening two verses of the chapter appear to convey a little prophecy complete in itself. The prophet is told to measure off the Temple at Jerusalem and its worshipers, in order that both may be protected in the coming time of trial (for the symbolism compare Ezek. 40:3 f and Amos 7:7 ff). The outer court of the Temple and the city itself are not to be measured, for they are given over to the Gentiles for destruction.

How are we to interpret this prophecy? It is my conviction that the book of Revelation is concerned with the church of Christ and the Jerusalem that comes down from heaven, not with the fortunes of the Jewish nation and its capital city. Whatever this prophecy may have meant to a non-Christian Jewish prophet, it is certain that John wishes us to interpret the picture figuratively. History had shown that the belief, frequently expressed by Jews, that Jerusalem and its Temple could not be taken by Gentile oppressors was false. At the time when John wrote his book the city and the Temple lay in ruins. In contrast to this John was certain —and he repeats it in all kinds of ways—that the church of Christ is indestructible, and that God himself will preserve it in face of the violent onslaughts of men who would blot it out from existence. This is what the little prophecy is intended by John to convey. It is not a promise that the church of Christ will be preserved from suffering. It is an assurance that the Lord's people can never perish. In face of overwhelming pressure of adversaries that is an important assurance for Christians to receive.

The next oracle (vv. 3–13) is more complicated. It is stated that in the period of trial (variously described as 1,260 days, 42 months, or 3½ years) two witnesses are appointed to prophesy, and their proclamation will be accompanied by portents in the heavens and on earth. Who are these witnesses? The description of their deeds—fire from their mouths to consume their enemies, power to shut up the sky that no rain may fall, power to turn water into blood and to strike the earth with every kind of plague—show that Moses and Elijah are in mind. The last paragraph of the Old Testament contains a prophecy that Elijah will return among men before the end comes (Mal. 4:5 f). A first-century Jewish rabbi has recorded a prophecy, as from the Lord to Moses, "If I send the prophet Elijah, you must both come together." It looks as though John has taken up an earlier Jewish oracle, which described the prophetic activity of Moses and Elijah in Jerusalem in the last days, and he has modified it to convey a quite new meaning.

Observe that the *two* witnesses are identified as the *two* olive trees and the *two* lamps which stand in the presence of the Lord of the earth (v. 4). This echoes the vision of Zechariah 4, where the two olive trees represent Joshua, the priest, and Zerubbabel, the governor; they supply the lamp, which denotes Israel, with oil that it may shine in the world for God. Here, however, the single lampstand of Zechariah becomes two. Why is this? It becomes two so as to accord with the two olive trees and the two witnesses. We recall that in the opening vision of the Revelation lamps represent the churches. As in that first vision the seven lamps represent the whole church in its diverse congregations, so in this passage the church is portrayed under the figure of the two lamps. The vision thereby yields the meaning that the function of prophecy, expected of Moses and Elijah at the end time, is given to the church of Christ. This is its task in the time of trial.

Because of the testimony borne by the church, the beast from the abyss wages war on the witnesses. No statement is given to explain who the beast is. He is mentioned without introduction in verse 7. Obviously everybody understands that he is the enemy of God, the antichrist. The war which he wages has fearful results: the witnesses will be killed, their corpses will lie in the street of the great city, and all on the earth will gloat over them. The description of the city is noteworthy: it is called "Sodom, or Egypt, the place where their Lord was crucified" (v. 8). By a single phrase the ancient city of God (Jerusalem) is equated with the city of greatest wickedness (Sodom) and the place of defiant resistance to God's will (Egypt). The threefold description conveys the notion of what Bunyan called Vanity Fair—the world that has no room for Christ. As Jerusalem crucified Christ, so the godless world murders his followers. The church of the Lamb who was slain walks the Via Dolorosa (the road from Pilate's judgment hall to the hill of Calvary) and endures a passion even as he did.

The end of the church's passion, like that of its Lord, is resurrection. "At the end of the three days and a half the breath of life from God came into them; and they stood up on their feet to the terror of all who saw it. . . . And they went up to heaven in a cloud, in full view of their enemies" (vv. 1 f). This language about the breath of God breathed into the saints, which enabled them to live and stand on their feet, comes from Ezekiel 37:10, where it refers to the spiritual quickening of the nation Israel. In this passage therefore the "resurrection" of the church could signify a revival so tremendous as to awe the world which witnesses it. It could equally relate to the resurrection and transformation of Christ's people at his coming, as in 1 Thessalonians 4 and 1 Corinthians 15. The matter is not of ultimate importance to decide, since the end of the age is immediately narrated in the vision, and the onset of the kingdom of God and of his Christ is celebrated in song (v. 15). The vindication of God's saints and their triumph over the forces of antichrist is complete. They enter with their Lord unto his victorious kingdom.

(3) Chapters 12—14 constitute the lengthiest parenthesis in the book. Their purpose is to reveal the nature of the conflict that is waged on earth. The struggle of the saints against the Caesars gives way to a vaster contest between the Lord of heaven and the powers of hell. From an understanding of the nature of the conflict Christians can draw strength to endure and conquer in their own field of battle.

The vision of chapter 12 describes the birth of a child from a woman robed with the sun with the moon beneath her feet and stars as her crown. A dragon waits to devour the child, but the child is snatched up to heaven. The woman flees into the wilderness and is hidden by God for the period of tribulation. War breaks out in heaven between the dragon and Michael and his angels. The dragon is defeated and is thrown down to earth. He makes war on the woman and her children, but they overcome him by "the blood of the Lamb and the testimony they declare."

An enormous amount of research has been devoted to the elucidation of this passage. John appears to have taken over and modified for his purpose an ancient story which was known over the world of his day. It was, so to say, his most famous cartoon. The Babylonians used to tell of the overthrow of the wicked sea monster Tiamat by the young god of heaven Marduk. The Persians spoke of the conflict between the good god Ormuzd and the evil Ahriman to secure the "kingly glory," and the evil Ahriman sent Azhi Dahak, the dragon, to seize it. The Egyptians told of the birth of the sun god Horus, whose mother was pursued by the evil dragon Typhon, and how Horus finally slew the dragon. The Greeks related how the great dragon sought to kill Leto, because her son was to destroy him, but four days after his birth Leto's son Apollo killed the dragon. Apparently this tradition had become international, and it embodied the universal longing for a deliverer who should redeem mankind from the powers that threaten it. For this reason it had been appropriated by a Jewish prophet, who affirmed that the real deliverer was the Messiah, assisted by Michael and his angels. John went a stage further and identified the Messiah with the Lord Jesus Christ. At a stroke, therefore, he declared that the hope of the world was fulfilled in Jesus, and all other names under heaven in which men have trusted are eliminated.

William Carey, Jr., caught the idea of the passage perfectly in his hymn, written for Indian Christians and which young British Baptists love to sing:

> Jesus only, none beside, He's the Saviour;
> Jesus only, none beside.

> Who is he will rescue me from this great load of sinning?
> Jesus only, none beside, He's the Saviour,
> Jesus only, none beside.

> Gods and goddesses throng us with promises,
> But they all will guilty fall 'neath their load of sinning.
> Jesus only, none beside, He's the Saviour,
> Jesus only, none beside.

Fathers and mothers love as no others,
But their care is vain to bear this your load of sinning.
    Jesus only, none beside, He's the Saviour,
    Jesus only, none beside.

Clasp the feet of Jesus, for 'tis he who frees us,
He has laid on his own head all your load of sinning.
    Jesus only, none beside, He's the Saviour,
    Jesus only, none beside.

The Christian hymn rejoices in Jesus as *savior* from sin and guilt. But where does that come in the original story? The answer is that it doesn't. Pagans do not know of a savior who bears our guilt in an all-sufficient sacrifice for sins. Their story said that the deliverer was snatched to heaven as soon as he was born. The fact that Jesus has ascended into heaven as Lord of the universe makes it possible to appropriate the original story. But the missing essential of the gospel is implied through the addition of the victor's song (v. 11): "By the sacrifice of the Lamb they have conquered him, and by the testimony which they uttered." They conquered because the Christ by his atoning death and mighty resurrection defeated the devil's claim to man, and believers share his victory as they confess the "testimony," that is the gospel. The accuser therefore has no room in heaven. He is thrown out to do his worst on earth.

There is an extraordinary parallel to this passage in John 12:31 f: "Now is the judgment of this world. Now shall the prince of this world be cast out, and I shall draw all men to myself, when I am lifted up from the earth." In the sacrificial death of Jesus and his enthronement at God's right hand the devil suffered a decisive defeat; henceforth the Savior draws to himself in heaven all who put their trust in him.

In the vision of Revelation 13, therefore, the dragon is helpless to harm believers. They are, as it were, sustained in the wilderness. It is an extraordinary picture. When the dragon wages his furious war against the saints they are as secure as if they were removed to another world. The hand of the Lord reaches down from heaven to cover those who maintain faith in him.

A fresh development occurs in chapter 13. The dragon, having been flung out of heaven, stands on the seashore and calls out of it a beast to help him. It is another form of the sea monster. John's readers would recognize the cartoon instantly: this second beast is the antigod empire personalized in its representative, the emperor. The leader of the empire is another manifestation of the devilish power that has opposed God throughout history.

Observe, however, what is said about this creature: "The beast was allowed to mouth bombast and blasphemy, and was given the right to reign for forty-two months. It opened its mouth in blasphemy against God, reviling his name and his heavenly dwelling. It was also allowed to wage war on God's people and to defeat them, and was granted authority over every tribe and people, language and nation. . . ." Now who "allowed" the beast to act in this way? Verse 4 could give the impression that it was the dragon who granted this power ("The dragon . . . had conferred his authority upon the beast"). But does the dragon set a limit of forty-two months on the beast's reign? Naturally not. That was God's appointed limit. The authority of the beast to blaspheme and make war on the saints can at most be derived from the devil in a proximate way. Ultimately it comes from God alone. In John's view it was the ultimate source of power which alone mattered. At the time of his raging, therefore, antichrist remains under the almighty hand of God. The same applies to every evil power of history. As Luther saw, even the devil must be seen as *God's* devil! He can never step beyond the bound set by God, nor frustrate his ultimate purpose. No other view is possible to one who believes in the God of the Bible.

A second beast comes to the aid of the first (13:11 ff). He has two horns like a lamb. He is a parody of the Lamb of God, the Word of God. This is the lamb of the devil, and he declares the word of the devil. There is little doubt as to what is in John's mind as he paints this picture. Just as the emperor of Rome in his day was heading for the role of antichrist by his claims to be the divine savior and lord of men, so the priesthood of the cult of the emperor was playing a demonic role in persuading men to pay honors to the divine emperor. Whereas the activity of this priesthood was limited at the time of writing, John saw a time when the whole world would be called on to yield allegiance to one who claimed to be the political and religious lord of men. Then people would have to decide whether they would follow the Christ of God or the Christ of the devil.

Something approximating this kind of claim and this kind of decision has more than once been presented to men in earlier generations, and perhaps never more pressingly than in our own, when the totalitarian claims of states have issued in the exaltation of a figure to whom something very close to religious veneration has been demanded and given. The people of God must be prepared for such an ultimatum, and stand steadfast for Christ at all costs.

Conclusion

Two issues are raised in the chapters we have been considering. The one relates to the church's task in the time of trial, the second to the role ascribed by John to the devil. We shall deal with the latter point first.

When talking about these chapters to a group of ministers, one requested of me, "Give us an 'Honest to the Devil.'" He was alluding to the book *Honest to God* and wanted an honest statement about the devil. That's a fair enough question, but it reflects the curious hesitation of the church today to commit itself to a clear attitude to a personal power of evil. Generally speaking the church tends to be unwilling to renounce belief in the devil absolutely but equally unwilling to affirm belief in the devil. Now John has more to say about the devil's action in the world than any other writer of the Bible. Was he simply a child of his time in taking over this belief, and is it one of those things which the modern Christian must reject, along with ideas about the earth being flat and the sun going round the globe?

Some Christian theologians unhesitatingly answer those questions in the affirmative. In their view the devil and demons are remnants of early mythological beliefs, attesting man's fear of the uncanny and his experience of evil. Man come of age must banish the devil from his thoughts.

I believe that this rejection is untenable to a Christian who takes revealed religion seriously. The following points need to be taken into account in discussion of the subject.

(1) Appeal to man's mythological beliefs about the supernatural is as strongly invoked to deny belief in God as it is to deny belief in the devil. People cite crude notions about God and use them to justify their rejection of the biblical teaching on God. We Christians protest that this disregards the revelation of God in history which culminates in Christ, and that it confounds distorted views of God with the reality they falsely interpret. The like holds good about the personal power of evil; for the biblical teaching concerning him is given in connection with the revelation of God in Christ.

(2) A factor which prompts men to disregard the concept of the devil is identical with that which leads to a light view of the atonement of Christ: in the words of Anselm, "You have not sufficiently considered the weight of sin." The Bible sees a factor in sin beyond anything man can contrive. Emil Brunner comments:

> The analysis of sin is confronted by the implications of the "daemonic," which it is impossible to understand on purely psychological or even collective psychological lines. . . . This daemonic-Satanic ground-tone belongs essentially to historical existence, even though it is not everywhere manifested in the historical process. It has the closest connection with being unto death. It is like a continuous and deep organ bourdon, above which the historical life that we know moves, and which unceasingly reverberates through other harmonies, at times drowning everything else, and remaining impervious to all human influences—just as much as physical death—not even apparently affected by that radical though concealed revolution which faith accomplishes at the heart of interior personal life.[3]

(3) The New Testament links the devil more commonly with Christ than it does with us. This applies to the evangelists' descriptions of the life of Jesus, to the words of Jesus himself, to the apostolic interpretation of the redemption of Christ in the Epistles, and to the book of Revelation in its portrayal of the end of the age. Especially important is the significance of the temptations of Jesus, recorded in the first three Gospels. Everyone recognizes that the tradition of the temptation goes back to Jesus himself. It was a conflict which he personally experienced. It had to be fought and won at the beginning of his ministry; it continued during his ministry (Luke 22:28), and it culminated in his final sufferings. Mark 3:27 indicates that the works of Jesus were dependent on his prior victory over the power of evil. Luke 10:18 vividly portrays the overthrow of Satan in the ministry of Jesus (and his apostles?). John 12:31 declares that the death and resurrection of Jesus constitute the decisive defeat and condemnation of the devil. I personally am unwilling to reject the interpretation by Jesus of his own ministry, and I question the freedom of those who preach his message to reject Jesus' interpretation of his ministry.

(4) If the death and resurrection of Jesus signify the defeat of the devil, the conclusion of the devil's operations awaits the completion of Christ's redemption at the end of the age. Till that time the parable of the tares in the field holds good (Matt. 13:24 ff). Its pertinence to life in this world is all too plain. Evil and good grow alongside each other till the final separation. Belief in the devil is not a luxury available to the man who can believe anything. It is a pointer to the seriousness of

existence in this world and a reminder of the necessity of grace for any who hope to follow in the footsteps of Jesus.

This leads to a consideration of the task of the church, as we see it in the book of Revelation. There is no doubt that this book was written above all to strengthen the "embattled church," as one has described it, and to enable it to survive the onslaught of an implacable foe. But chapter 11 teaches that even in the time of antichrist the church has a greater duty than simply to survive. The church is called to bear witness to the world, even though it has to die for it. Indeed, the church will suffer, precisely because it does bear witness.

Now this is not a new insight. It is part of our Christian faith, that the church has been raised up for witness to the gospel of Christ. Nevertheless it is easy for us to forget that this has not always been self-evident in the church. And it is just as easy to overlook that in the New Testament, witness to Christ goes hand in hand with suffering for his name.

The first intimation of the church's duty to preach the gospel to the whole world is not in the resurrection commission but in our Lord's discourse about the end of the age. In Mark 13:9 ff we read:

> You will be handed over to the courts. You will be flogged in synagogues. You will be summoned to appear before governors and kings on my account, to testify in their presence. But before the end the gospel must be proclaimed to all nations. So when you are arrested and taken away, do not worry beforehand about what you will say, but when the

time comes say whatever is given to you to say, for it is not you who will be speaking, but the Holy Spirit.

This passage is by no means solitary, and it indicates that for Jesus evangelism and opposition are inseparable. That was also the experience of the earliest church, as the Acts of the Apostles illustrates again and again.

In the New Testament therefore he who bears witness to Christ must expect to suffer with Christ. Whereas, however, the burden of Jesus was, "You must witness, even though you will suffer for it," John the prophet urges, "You must suffer, but you must continue to bear witness even when you do suffer." Both emphases are equally strange to many in the modern church, though for some they are daily bread. When the church listens to Jesus, and to John, perhaps it will be able to look on much that has been happening in the world of our times with understanding. It will not be surprised, for example, at what has overtaken the church in the U.S.S.R., in China, and now in India, and elsewhere. How should the church expect to carry out its commission without opposition? In reality it has never done so for long. But neither can the church cease from its task when it is confronted by bayonets or the like. For no one needs the gospel more than its opponents. It was while we were *enemies* that Christ died for us. And Christ died for the allies of antichrist as truly as for his crucifiers. To such the word of judgment will be preached—and the word of grace.

The book of Revelation is full of the judgments of the Lord. But, as Matthias Rissi observed, "All the visions of judgment, which stand under the divine 'must,' have a very evident 'if not' before them." [4] That is, the proclamation of judgment is to warn men, that judgment may be averted if they repent.

That mercy may be upon all is the purpose of witnessing to Christ in the first age, and in the last age, and in all the generations between them.

Chapter 4
The Dark Side of Hope: The Judgment of the Nations

Revelation 6—9,15—19

The belief that the revelation of the final kingdom of God will be preceded by an overwhelming manifestation of the judgments of God is rooted in the teaching of the Old Testament prophets. Amos pronounced woe on his contemporaries who looked forward to the day of the Lord; for people with religion but no righteousness the day of the Lord is "darkness, and not light" (Amos 5:18 ff). This teaching is devastatingly developed in the book of Zephaniah. He begins his prophecies with a pronouncement of doom:

> I will sweep the earth clean of all that is on it, says the Lord
> I will sweep away both man and beast,
> I will sweep the birds from the air and the fish from the sea.
>   and I will bring the wicked to their knees
>   and wipe out mankind from the earth.
> This is the very word of the Lord.

He then describes the day of the Lord in these terms:

That day is the day of wrath,
A day of anguish and affliction,
A day of destruction and devastation,
A day of murk and gloom,

A day of cloud and dense fog,
A day of trumpet and battle cry
   over fortified cities and lofty battlements.
I will bring dire distress upon men;
They shall walk like blind men for their sin against the Lord (Zeph. 1:2 ff,15 ff).

Jesus does not speak at length concerning the circumstances of the coming of the Kingdom, but there are passages of his teaching (e.g., in Mark 13; Matt. 24; Luke 21) in which he endorses the characteristic prophetic teaching on the signs that precede the end of the age. It is significant that in his opening description of the judgments of the end (the series of seven seals, Rev. 6—8) John closely adheres to the teaching of the Lord's discourse on Olivet.

There is, however, much more to follow in the book of Revelation, above all the judgments of the seven trumpets and the seven bowls of wrath. Does John intend us to understand his long descriptions of judgment as one continuous stream of events? Many expositors believe that such is his intention. I myself do not accept that view. That John's prophecies, contained in chapters 6—19 of his book, do not describe a chain of events in unbroken chronological order seems clearly indicated by his insertion of the vision of the woman and the child in chapter 12, which relates to the birth of the Messiah and the redemption he achieved through his death and ascension to the throne of God. It appears to me beyond contradiction that *an identical point of time is reached at the end of each series of judgments depicted under the symbols of the seven seals, seven trumpets, and seven bowls; that point is the coming of the kingdom of God.*

In the case of the seven seals this feature has been obscured by the separation of the description of the sixth seal from that of the seventh by an interlude in chapter 7; it is one of the many in John's book which assure the people of God that they have nothing to fear from these judgments. The sixth seal leads to signs of cosmic catastrophe which the Old Testament prophets always associate with the coming of the kingdom: "The sun turned black as a funeral pall, and the moon all red as blood; the stars in the sky fell to the earth, like figs shaken down by a gale; the sky vanished, as a scroll is rolled up, and every mountain and island was moved from its place. Then the kings of the earth called out to the mountains and the crags: 'Fall on us and hide us from the face of the One who sits on the throne and from the vengeance of the Lamb.' For the great day of their vengeance has come, and who will be able to stand" (6:12 ff). Clearly this is the end of history. There is nothing much that can happen after that, other than the unveiling of the king in his kingdom. The seventh seal therefore leads to silence in heaven, followed by thunder, lightning, and an earthquake, such as we find occurring after the seven trumpets and seven bowls as immediate precursors of the end of this age.

Similarly after the sounding of the seventh trumpet voices in heaven proclaim, "The sovereignty of the world has passed to our Lord and his Christ, and he shall reign for ever and ever." The elders in their worship declare, "Thou hast taken thy great power into thy hands and entered upon thy reign"; then follow thunder, lightning, and an earthquake (11:14–19). So also after the pouring out of the seventh bowl a loud voice came from the throne of God which said, "It is over." There followed lightning, thunder, and a violent earthquake, in which the cities of the world fell in ruin. John is then given to see how the antigod city is overthrown, to hear the hallelujahs of heaven at the coming of the kingdom, and to view the Lord coming in glory (chaps. 17—19).

It is important that we should recognize John's procedure in his prophecies. He is not piling on agony after agony in a meaningless profusion of torments. He characterizes the period of the last tribulation from a series of different viewpoints.

There is an extraordinary precedent for this in the doom prophecy of Leviticus 26. Four times over it is declared that if Israel is rebellious, "I will multiply your calamities seven times, as your sins deserve" (see vv. 18,21,24,28). If John needed any encouragement to systematize the well-known messianic judgments, it is here given in the Bible. The "seven times" of Leviticus 26 are variously represented by John as the effects of God's will and testament being opened in order that the kingdom might come; as the last trumpets sounding out the doom that leads to the resurrection; and as the cups of God's wrath meted out to the wicked before the cup of blessing is given to the righteous in final salvation. By this triplication of the sevenfold chastisement the prophet builds up to a tremendous and awe-inspiring climax, which befits the grandeur of his theme. By the time the coming of the Lord arrives, we really are ready for him!

These pictures of judgment we shall now briefly review.

I. The Seven Seals: Revelation 6:1 to 8:5

For the form of the opening four judgments of the seals, John has adapted a vision of Zechariah 6 and combined it with the thought of Ezekiel 14:12–21. (Note that the repeated "Come" of verses 1,3,5,7 is said to the riders, not to John. The words of the Authorized Version "and see" are an addition of a later scribe, and are omitted in recent translations.)

Revelation 6:1. The first rider on a white horse is often identified with Christ, simply because he goes forth "conquering and to conquer." But a series of judgments is being depicted. The rider represents a conquering power of the last days, invading many territories.

Verse 3. The second rider creates strife, including apparently both international and civil war.

Verse 5. The third rider brings famine, for the prices quoted are prohibitive (6:6). A penny was a day's wages; a measure of wheat sufficed for one person for one day; three measures of barley still represent a bare subsistence allowance. "Hurt not the oil and wine" presupposes ample supplies of less needed goods.

Verse 7. The fourth rider represents death. Hades that follows serves to remind that judgment follows death as well as precedes it.

Verse 9. The fifth seal reveals the souls of the martyrs. They were under the altar because they had been sacrificed. Theirs was a position of honor, not of humiliation. The well-known Jewish teacher Rabbi Akiba said:

"Whoever was buried in the land of Israel was just as if he were buried under the altar, and whoever was buried under the altar was as if he were buried under the throne of glory." The prayer of the martyrs was a judgment as truly as anything that has gone before, for it hastens the end (8:1–5).

Verses 12 ff. The sixth seal is followed by an earthquake and cosmic signs that herald the day of the wrath of the Lamb.

Revelation 8:1–5. The seventh seal is followed by silence. Why? A Jewish tradition states: "In the fifth heaven are companies of angels of service who sing praises by night but are silent by day because of the glory of Israel"; i.e., they are silent that Israel's praises may be heard. In our text heaven is quieted to hear not praises, but cries for deliverance from suffering Christians on earth (8:4). Their prayers are followed by the signs of the end (8:5). The kingdom therefore finally comes through prayer (Compare Luke 18:2–8).

II. The Seven Trumpets: Revelation 8:6 to 11:19

As the seven seals fall into two groups of four and three, so the seven trumpets divide themselves in a similar fashion. The first four have distinct reminiscences of the Egyptian plagues at the Exodus. In Revelation 15:3 the second coming of Christ is tacitly compared with the Exodus. Accordingly it is heralded by like plagues on the ungodly.

Observe that none of the woes concerns the church directly. Martin Kiddle suggests that this passage is John's equivalent of Paul's indictment of the world in Romans 1.

The Judgment of the Nations

Revelation 8:7. The first trumpet brings fire on a third of the earth. Compare the plague of hail and fire in Exodus 9:23 ff.

Verse 8. The second trumpet brings destruction on the sea and a third of it turns to blood. Compare the turning of the river to blood in Exodus 7:20 f.

Verse 10. The third trumpet poisons a third of fresh waters, so continuing the previous plague.

Verse 12. The fourth trumpet darkens a third of the heavens. This corresponds to the Egyptian plague of darkness (Ex. 10:21 ff).

Revelation 9:1. The fifth trumpet brings a plague of demonic locusts (Compare Joel 2:10). They torment the men who have not the seal of God in their foreheads. The description in this and the following plague is highly imaginative. It is possible that in both of them John wishes to suggest the troubling of humanity by demonic powers.

Verses 13 ff. The sixth trumpet brings a demonic army from the river Euphrates—two hundred million of them! This river formed the ideal limit of the land of Israel (Gen. 15:18). Beyond it lay the empires of Babylon and Assyria. As armies came from these unknown territories to ravage disobedient Israel of old, so would more terrifying hordes arise to punish the godless world. The description of verses 17 f recall the monsters of heathen mythology. John indicates that this hellish crowd beggars the most terrifying imagination of pagan superstition.

Revelation 11:15 f. The seventh trumpet is followed by the coming of the kingdom of God. The revelation of the ark of the covenant in heaven (v. 19) implies that the goal of the covenant is now being realized in the giving of the kingdom.

III. The Seven Bowls: Revelation 15—16

The bowls are intended to recall the cups of wrath of which the Old Testament prophets often spoke as handed by God to the nations (see e.g. Isa. 51:17–23; Jer. 25:15–29). They initiate "seven plagues, the last plagues of all, for with them the wrath of God is consummated" (v. 1).

They do this in that they culminate what has gone before and include the final blows against the wickedness of an age that has gone to the devil.

The contents of the seven bowls are similar to those of the seven trumpets. In most cases they amplify the earlier plagues. Thus they give a fuller revelation of what has been shown under the trumpet judgments, together with certain new features.

The conquerors sing by the sea of glass a song of victory, as Israel sang beside the Red Sea after their deliverance. This song celebrates the approaching conversion of the nations after the completion of the "righteous acts of God" (v. 4).

Revelation 16:2. The first bowl is poured out on earth. Sores fall on the servants of the Beast. (Compare Exodus 9:10–11.)

Verse 3. The second bowl is poured on the sea. Whereas the second trumpet affected a third of the sea, this spreads through all the seas.

Verse 4. The third bowl falls on the rivers and springs. The same plague is in mind.

Verse 8. The fourth bowl is poured on the sun. It

scorches men with intense heat.

Verse 10. The fifth bowl is poured on the realm of the beast, so that it suffers darkness, and men suffer more sores and pains. (Compare Exodus 10:21.) Are we intended to think of the further effect of the fifth trumpet—the demon locusts from the abyss? (See 9:1 ff.)

Verse 12. The sixth bowl is poured on the river Euphrates, just as the sixth trumpet affected the same river. The water is dried up to allow the kings of the east to invade the west. These latter are described further in 17:12 ff. The kings of the earth are prepared for the battle of Armageddon. It would appear that we are not to think of a geographical spot. It is an *occasion* that is in mind, namely the last rebellion that precedes the kingdom of God.

Verse 17. The seventh bowl is poured on the air, and the end comes. The cities of the nations fall, and Babylon is remembered by God: she is made to drink the cup filled with the fierce wine of God's anger. Every island and every mountain vanishes.

IV. The Fall of Babylon: Revelation 17:1 to 19:10

"Babylon was remembered by God" (16:19). This is the theme of the chapters which lead to the description of the Lord's coming in glory. In them we are taken back to a point in time prior to the end of the drama, in order that we may learn what happens to the antichristian power in the close of the age.

John's vision portrays a woman gorgeously dressed, mounted on a scarlet beast which had seven heads and ten horns. The woman is called "Babylon the Great, the mother of whores and of every obscenity on earth," and she is drunk with the blood of God's people.

John is once more using and adapting the ancient cartoon of the primeval monster. The woman and the beast go back to a single symbol, for originally the monster of the sea was thought of as female. John employs the two forms of the tradition, for they well set forth the idea of an antigod city ruling an antigod empire, both of which are devilish.

The woman is a new Babylon, sharing a nature like that of the city against which the prophets of former days prophesied. In the interpretation of his vision John explicitly states that the woman is "the great city that holds sway over the kings of the earth" (v. 18). Which city does he have in mind? The answer is indicated in one of the two interpretations he gives of the seven heads. "The seven heads are seven hills on which the woman sits" (v. 9). This description clearly designates Rome, which was commonly known as the city of the seven hills. Rome was the new Babylon of John's day.

John then gives a second meaning to the seven heads of the beast (v. 10). They represent seven kings, of whom five have gone before, one is reigning at the time of the writing, and another is to come for a short time. We may take it that the sixth king has only a short time to go. The seventh is explicitly stated to reign for a short while. Who comes after this last one? John answers in a riddle: "The beast that once was alive and is alive no longer, he is an eighth, and yet he is one of the seven, and he is going to perdition." The riddle is not difficult for John's readers. It was the old cartoon with a very topical application. According to the ancient tradition the wicked power of ancient times had been overcome by the Lord of heaven, but it would raise its head again; so John could say of the beast that it *was,* i.e., it had once been active; it *is not*—i.e., it is at present subdued; but it *is to be,* i.e., it will be active again. In plainer speech it might be said that the devilish influence which had used political powers from time to time in history was about to become incarnate in a final manifestation of wickedness. But it would be active not alone in the corporate life of a *city* and *empire;* the empire in all its wickedness would become embodied in the person of one of its kings, who had a history like the beast itself: the antichristian *ruler* himself "was, and is not, but is to come."

It is possible that in this language John is alluding to current beliefs about the emperor Nero. We know that an extraordinary development took place in the latter half of the first century A.D. regarding the popular image of Nero. As the most hated of all emperors he had instilled a deep fear into people. When it was first spread abroad that Nero was dead, the news was not believed, and more than one imposter appeared in the empire claiming to be Nero yet alive. When at length it became clear that Nero had died, the belief arose that he would return from the dead to wreak vengeance on the people. This idea actually appears in two Jewish works of this period, the Ascension of Isaiah and the Sibylline Oracles, in which Nero figures as the antichrist.

Did John, then, instruct people to expect that Nero would personally come from the hellish underworld to work as the devil's instrument in the world? No, I do not believe that he did, any more than that he considered that the city of Rome was a woman in whom the sea monster Tiamat had come to life again. What John has done is to take the two cartoons—one ancient and the other "modern"—and bring them together to show his contemporaries the fate of those who play the role of the enemies of the Lord of heaven and earth: they must suffer destruction from the Lord they fight.

It so happens that John himself has given us an instructive parallel to his method in this chapter. We have already noticed that the Old Testament closes with the promise that Elijah will be sent before the day of the Lord comes (Mal. 4:5–6). Jesus himself cited this prophecy and told his disciples that Elijah had come in their lifetime in John the Baptist. He did not mean by this that John the Baptist was a reincarnation of Elijah but that John was, as it were, another Elijah. Indeed, in the angelic message to John's mother Elizabeth it was said, "He will go before [the Lord] as forerunner, possessed by the spirit and power of Elijah" (Luke 1:17). We have further seen that the author of the book of Revelation uses this Elijah prophecy in yet another way: the whole church fulfils the prophesied ministry of Elijah by its witness in word and deed (chap. 11). In a similar way it would seem that John utilized the widespread idea that Nero would return as a demonic spirit: the antichrist will be a devilish agent, who will, as it were, work "by the spirit and power of Nero." In this way he fulfils the ancient picture of the evil power that has resisted the God of heaven from of old. He becomes the embodiment of the evil experienced by God's people throughout the ages and which is expected in the future.

Ironically, however, John shows that the antichrist destroys not the people of God but the persecuting power itself—the city drunk with the blood of the martyrs (Rev. 17:15–17). So the strange thing comes to pass, that the instrument of divine judgment upon the antichrist-city is the antichrist-ruler. The devil topples his own house into ruin.

It is this event which is celebrated in chapter 18, which is a dirge over godless Babylon, modeled on the doom songs of the Old Testament prophets over the hostile nations of their own times. It summarizes all the prophetic oracles on the doom of unrighteous peoples. The prophecies against Babylon (compare Isa. 13; 27; 47 and Jer. 50—51) and against Tyre (Ezek. 26—27) were especially in John's mind. The eternal ruin of the city of antichrist forms a vivid contrast to the eternal glory of the city of God, which is described a little later (chaps. 21—22).

What are we to say of the fact that the city of Rome did not, in fact, fall to destruction, but actually became a center of Christian faith for the world? Was John mistaken about his belief in antichrist and the judgment of the world, and about his belief in the vindication of the church and the victory of Christ? Certainly not. John did what all the prophets of the Bible had done. They set the day of the Lord in relation to their own day and so the events of their day in juxtaposition with the day of judgment and the coming of the kingdom. The expectation of a culmination of wickedness on earth, in a great resistance to Christ and his kingdom through antichrist and his realm, is part of the biblical faith. John saw that Rome actually was beginning to play the part of antichrist. As the outcome of the tendencies then at work was that which the former prophets had spoken of, he applied his visions to his situation. The stage was set for the end, and John described the drama. On the canvas of his age he pictured the last great crisis of the world, not merely because from a psychological viewpoint he could do no other, but because of the real correspondence between his crisis and that of the last days. As the church was faced with a devastating persecution by Rome, so will the church of the last days find itself violently opposed by the world power. The outcome of that great struggle will be judgment on the resisting power and the establishment of God's kingdom in Christ's great advent. That this did not come to pass in the first century does not invalidate the essential nature of John's prophecy, any more than was the case with the other prophets of the Bible, from whom the intermediary stages of history were hidden. The many antichrists since John's day have increasingly approximated to his portrait and, we believe, will culminate in one who will suit it perfectly.

The doom song of chapter 18 is followed in chapter 19 with a series of hallelujahs from heaven for the justice of God in destroying the power that corrupted the earth. It is characteristic of the book of Revelation that the unveiling of God's judgments on the wicked is offset by representations of worship offered to God by the company of heaven and redeemed humanity. The theme of such worship is usually the judgments that have been described (see for example 7:9 f after the judgments of the seals, 11:15 f after the trumpets, 14:1 ff after the ravaging of antichrist). So in this passage the angels and the redeemed children of God unite in praise to God for his judgments on earth and because his kingdom has come:

> 'Alleluia! Victory and glory and power belong to our God, for true and just are his judgments!'
> 'Alleluia! The smoke goes up from her for ever and ever!'
> 'Amen! Alleluia'
> 'Alleluia! The Lord our God, sovereign over all, has entered on his reign! Exult and shout for joy and do him homage, for the wedding-day of the Lamb has come!'

Conclusion

The passages of Scripture which we have considered have some important lessons to teach us, lessons which are not altogether congenial to the modern mind.

(1) The presence of a doctrine of antichrist in the Bible is a sharp reminder of the limitations of what the best of men, including the church of God, can achieve this side of the last advent of Christ. We are sometimes inclined to think that the faithful preaching of the gospel and the loving service of humanity by the church are all that is needed for the conversion of the world. Certainly the church of Christ can never give less than these things. But to believe that these will of themselves overcome all the evil in the world is plain unrealism with regard to life, and it entails a plain rejection of a large slice of the Bible.

Emil Brunner, with his usual sense of balance, once said: "It is ingratitude and a sign of faltering faith in God not to reckon with the progress of the work of Christ in history; but it is childish folly and disobedience to Scripture to be unwilling to recognize the counteraction of evil and the limits of the progress of the Kingdom of Christ." [1] Alongside that I would set the dictum of Paul Althaus, one of the most profound writers of all time on the doctrine of the last things: "The concept of antichrist is a loud no to all secular Chiliasm, and to the optimistic faith in a progressive coming of the kingdom of God on earth." [2] The church must not forget this sobering thought as it contemplates its task in the world and endeavors to carry it out. There are some things which only God can do. One of them is to provide an atonement for evil, and another is to put a stop to the progress of evil, and they are not the same thing. In both respects God works through Christ. We may be grateful that he will achieve the second so sure as he has done the first through his Son. Part of the importance of the book of Revelation is its teaching on God's intention to do this very thing.

(2) A second contribution of these chapters of the Revelation is their emphasis on God's intention to judge the world, even in the course of its history, as well as beyond it. For judgment is as real an element of God's action in the world as sin is real in the world.

It is typical of contemporary man to be reluctant to recognize the reality and the gravity of judgment. What we said above about the doctrine of antichrist applies a hundredfold with regard to this matter. One needs only open eyes on the world and the open pages of the Bible to see the truth about sin and judgment.

We must never overlook the fact that the sin of man and the judgment of God are related both in the cross

The Judgment of the Nations

of Christ and in the coming of Christ. Perhaps this is why the theme of judgment is plainest in the Gospel of John, which is supremely a book of the passion of Christ, and the book of Revelation, which is above all the book about the coming of Christ.

Precisely in John 3:16 the love of God and the judgment of God come together in such a manner that neither eradicates the other, and to attempt the eradication is to falsify the gospel. It is none other than Rudolf Bultmann who draws from John 3:16 the lesson that the mission of Christ means life and judgment, and that since this event is grounded in the love of God it follows that God's love is the origin of the judgment. Moreover with the mission of Christ the judgment becomes a present reality in the world, so sure as the saving life of Christ is a present reality in the world. Bultmann is insistent that the message of God's love in Christ does not permit a rationalistic or a sentimental view of God, but on the contrary brings out the notion of judgment in its full force.

Now if the love and the judgment of God in Christ are presented with a fine balance in the Gospel of John, it must be admitted that the love of God is less conspicuous in the book of Revelation than his judgment. It would be false to assert that God's love is absent from the Revelation, for after all the closing chapters of the book give a vision of the city of God wherein the love of God is poured out on man in what can only be described as divine extravagance. Nevertheless the dark side of hope is the prominent note of this book. It was the contention of H. B. Swete that it had to be so, and that it was of the divine ordering that it was so.

Like the solemn descriptions of Godhead in the Hebrew prophets, it is an answer to the inanities of heathenism rather than a call to fellowship with the living God. A revelation of the 'severity of God' was needed by churches, which were hard pressed by the laxity of pagan life and the claims to divine honours made by the masters of the Empire. The Apocalyptist meets the immoralities and blasphemies of heathendom by a fresh setting forth of the majesty of the One God and a restatement of his sole right to the worship of men. Thus he represents a view of the Divine Character which, apart from his book would be nearly wanting in the New Testament, and supplies a necessary complement to the gentler teaching of the Gospels and Epistles.[3]

If this is true, it is necessary for us to give heed to the message of judgment contained in the Book of Revelation, for only so can we gain a full understanding of the revelation of God in the Bible.

(3) One final word. Martin Buber, the Jew, in a remarkable piece of writing reflected on the contribution of the Jewish people to the Christian church. "Divided from you," he said, "we have been assigned to you for your help." In what way can the Jew help the Christian? By reminding the church that it has not all in its possession and that there is a future before it. He cites his fellow Jew Rosenzweig: "You who live in an ecclesia triumphans need a silent servant, who reminds you every time you believe you have partaken of God in bread and wine, 'Sir, remember the last things' "[4] That is, *remember the judgment!* This service Israel can do for the Church, for Israel has borne judgment, and yet is still in the hand of God.

This is a solemn word, and a needful one. For while the book of Revelation is especially concerned with the judgments of God on the rebellious world, these things were written that the children of God should not be condemned with the world but enter the kingdom prepared for them. We do well to ponder the words of Peter, "The time has come for the judgment to begin; it is beginning with God's own household; and if it is starting with you, how will it end for those who refuse to obey the gospel of God?" (1 Pet. 4:15 f). It is a strange fact that these words were directed to the churches in the very area to which the book of Revelation was sent. The apostle who penned them called for a life consonant with the expectation of judgment. In gratitude for mercy already shown us in Christ, and in assurance of the mercy of God in his judgment, we too, should pursue our course with "fear and trembling," knowing that it is God who works in us both to will and to do his good pleasure (Phil. 2:12–13).

Chapter 5
The Goal of Hope: The Coming of Christ and His Kingdom

Revelation 19:11 to 22:21

I. The Coming of Christ: Revelation 19:11–21

The picture of Christ on a white horse, leading the armies of heaven to battle, is the one unmistakable representation of the second advent of Christ in the book of Revelation. It is strange that this book of the last things of history is so full of Christ, and speaks so often of the coming of the kingdom of God, yet gives so little space to the actual event of the appearing of Christ. When it does describe the event, it deliberately uses impressionist effects. The Word of God, who is King of kings and Lord of lords, rides on a white horse. He is followed by the armies of heaven, also riding on horses. Are these armies of angels or of the saints of God? We cannot be sure, but in either case we can hardly think of them as taking a multitude of winged horses out of heavenly stables and riding down the skies to meet the massed forces of antichrist on earth. The horses are as real as the blood-dipped robe of the risen Christ, as real as the winepress he treads, as real as the sword which sticks out of his mouth, as real as the letters imprinted on his thigh, as real as the birds which gorge themselves on human flesh, as real as the brimstone in the lake of fire. The whole picture is imaginative, and it is intended so to be understood.

It is important to be clear about this, not merely to make sense of the narrative but above all to ensure that we do not mistake its purpose. For it is easy to confuse the fact that the prophet paints the advent of Christ in the colors of a warrior riding to battle with the idea that the risen Lord appears among men in order to wage a war. Christ does not come for war. There is no battle when he appears. There is a revelation of his glory and an act of judgment. The sole weapon he possesses is the sword of his mouth, by which the will of God is declared and thereby performed. At the end, as at the beginning, the Word of God speaks, and it is done.

The chief point of John's picture, therefore, is that the Lord, whose real name is unknown, whose power is limitless and whose sovereignty is universal, reveals that sovereignty at the God-ordained time and makes it effective in the universe. The revelation is *action*—a declaration of "thus far and no further" to the destructive powers in God's world.

For the completeness of the picture it must be observed that the armies of heaven come dressed in white: they come prepared for a wedding! The day when the King of kings utters his word of judgment in earth's gladdest day; the Church enters on its reign with Christ, and the world enters upon its emancipation from the powers of evil.

II. The Kingdom of Christ in History: Revelation 20

At this point in John's book the disclosure of the long-awaited kingdom is given. At least, this was the common interpretation in the early centuries of the church, and this is the usual interpretation in modern critical exposition. Some expositors, however, have felt justified in adopting a different understanding of chapter 20 popularized by Augustine. Fundamentally it involves the idea that this chapter does not continue the narrative beyond the second advent of Christ. It is held that the opening verse goes back to the beginning of the church's story, so that it describes not the final kingdom but the age of the church. On this basis the binding of Satan in 20:1-3 is identified with the ejection of Satan from heaven in 12:9; the thousand years of the church's reign in 20:4-6 are paralleled with its period of witness described in chapter 11; and the onset of Gog and Magog in 20:7 ff is equated with the persecution of antichrist described in the earlier chapters.

We all have to make up our minds about this issue. I believe this view is mistaken for three reasons.

(1) In 12:9 Satan is ejected from *heaven,* where he can no longer accuse the saints before God, owing to the all-sufficient sacrifice of Christ; and so he rampages on *earth* and makes war on the saints. In chapter 20 he is removed from the earth and packed off to the *"abyss,"* where he is powerless to affect those who dwell on earth. Admittedly John is using symbolism, but he intends to convey meaning through the medium of his pictures. For him the abyss is what is popularly termed hell, and even in the book of Revelation heaven, earth, and hell are viewed as different spheres!

(2) Revelation 20:1-3 continues the description of the conquest of God's enemies begun in the preceding

paragraph of 19:20–21. In the last two verses of chapter 19 the antichrist and the false prophet are taken and thrown into the lake of fire. In 20:1 ff their leader, the devil, is seized and chained in the abyss. This trinity of evil is grouped together in 16:13, and it is clear that they are similarly bracketed together in this passage. The narrative therefore is continuous. It is our late chapter division which is responsible for obscuring this fact, but John must not be blamed for that.

(3) In Revelation 12:9 Satan's time to work on earth is said to be "short," and for this reason he furiously rages. In chapter 20 he is locked below for a thousand years. A short time on earth in which to be angry is hardly to be equated with a thousand years to cool off in hell! Now this is more serious than it may at first sound. The whole book of Revelation reflects the conviction that the end is to come "shortly." (See for example 1:3, "the hour of fulfilment is near;" 22:20, "I am coming soon.") Such a viewpoint is characteristic of prophets both in the Old and New Testaments. The term "prophetic perspective" has been coined for it: the prophet views the mountaintops of God's saving and judging action but not the extent of the valleys lying between the peaks. It is inconceivable that John could have expressed himself as he has done about the end coming "soon" if he believed that the church had a thousand years (or even thousands, if the number is purely symbolical) before the second coming of Christ. No writer in the New Testament held such a view, nor did John.

For these reasons I believe that we must accept the book of Revelation as looking for a realization of the triumphant kingdom of Christ on earth, after the coming of Christ and prior to the eternal state in the new creation. The significance of this datum we shall consider later.

The limits of the description of the millennium in John's book are uncertain. The suggestion has been made (by such different commentators as William Kelly of the Plymouth Brethren, the German New Testament scholar Theodore Zahn, and the British expert on apocalyptic writings R. H. Charles) that the description of the city of God in chapters 21—22 largely relates to the millennial kingdom.

Charles adduced three reasons for his view: [1]

(1) Revelation 21:24 ff seems to presuppose a continuation of earthly conditions. Nations receive blessings from the city, kings bring their glory to it, and the unclean are denied access to it.

(2) The leaves of the tree of life are for the healing of the nations. This is a difficult figure to apply to risen humanity in Christ's image in a heavenly existence.

(3) Blessing is pronounced (in 22:14) on those who have right to the tree of life and enter the city, and a warning is given that evildoers will be kept outside it.

More important than these considerations is the indubitable fact that in chapter 20 the hosts of Gog and Magog lay siege to "the camp of God's people and the city that he loves" (20:9). This indicates plainly that the city is accessible in the millennial kingdom.

It should further be observed that the promises to the victors, which conclude each of the seven letters, chiefly relate to life in the city of God. In Revelation 2:26 ff this has to do with participating in the millennial rule; in 3:12 it explicitly refers to having part in the new Jerusalem. This suggests at least that life in the city which descends from God embraces both the millennium and the new creation. The city of God is the dwelling of God's people in the kingdom of Christ and in the eternal kingdom.

If these arguments are not compelling, they are certainly very plausible. It is at least an interesting possibility—and I would say a likely one—that Revelation 20:1 to 22:5 gives a condensed narrative of events set in motion by the coming of the Lord and that 21:9 ff provides a description of the city of God which will be the eternal home of the people of God, alike in the millennium and in the new creation.

There is a further point of debate in the understanding of Revelation 20 which should at least be looked at. Who are the people who occupy the thrones in verse 4? John writes in verses 4–5: "I could see the souls of those who had been beheaded for the sake of God's word and their testimony to Jesus, (and) those who had not worshipped the beast and its image or received its mark on foreheads or hand. These came to life again and reigned with Christ for a thousand years, though the rest of the dead did not come to life until the thousand years were over. This is the first resurrection." From this statement it is widely concluded that the martyrs *alone* rise to participate in the millennium. The rest of the Christian dead are then excluded from the first resurrection, and of course believers who may have survived the onslaughts of antichrist.

Now this interpretation has always seemed difficult to me. The whole book of Revelation resounds with assurances to believers that they will participate in Christ's kingdom at his coming. This is the burden of the promises to the victors in the seven letters. The new song, sung when the Lamb takes the book of God's testament to put it into effect, celebrates the creation of the church to be a "royal house, to serve our God as priests, and they shall reign on earth" (5:9 f). So also, at the conclusion of the messianic judgments, a vast crowd shouts in exultation: "Alleluia! the Lord our God, sovereign over all, has entered on his reign. Exult and shout for joy and do him homage, for the wedding day of the Lamb has come! His bride has made herself ready . . ." (19:6 ff). There can be no doubt that for John the bride is the church in its entirety, not a part of it. The marriage takes place at Christ's coming for the millennial rule. Accordingly we may say that in 20:4 John singles out the martyrs for special mention and consolation, but we must insist they are not viewed as the exclusive heirs of the kingdom of Christ.

III. The New Creation: Revelation 21:1 ff

The creation of a new heaven and a new earth is taught in Isaiah 65:17; 66:22. It is implied by our Lord in Mark 13:31 and vividly pictured in 2 Peter 3:12. It finds frequent mention in the apocalyptic writings. The latter, however, push to an extreme a thought latent in this doctrine, that the present creation (or at least its present form) is insufficient to be the scene of the perfected eternal kingdom of God.

The assertion that the sea is no more has in mind the personification of the sea as the quintessence of evil. Whatever else is meant, therefore, the main sentiment is the exclusion of evil from the new order of existence.

The central element in the new blessedness of creation is given in verse 3: "Now at last God has his dwelling among men! He will dwell among them and they shall be his people, and God himself will be with them." The picture of the dwelling of God among the pilgrim people in the desert and the visitation of the Shekinah glory in history and in the temple are eclipsed by the final reality of the unveiled glory among men.

"God himself will be with them" echoes the name Emmanuel, God with us. He was with us temporarily in the flesh. He is with us invisibly in the Spirit. He will be with us manifestly in glory at the end.

IV. The City of God: Revelation 21:9 ff

This vision opens in an extraordinary manner: "Come, and I will show you the bride, the wife of the Lamb. . . . He showed me the holy city of Jerusalem coming down out of heaven from God." The bride is a city. The city is the wife of the Lamb. Apart from the fact that this provides a clear instance of John's ability drastically to change his imagery, it shows that the city is the church, and this must be borne in mind in reading the description that follows.

Verse 11 f. The city shines with the glory of God and has the radiance of jasper. In Revelation 4:3 the appearance of God in vision is as jasper. The city of God thus shares the likeness of God, reflecting his very nature in its being. This represents the consummation of God's work in his church. (See 1 John 3:2.)

Verse 12. The city has a wall—144 cubits—216 feet! But the translation must not be made, the 12 by 12 must be kept. The wall signifies strength for the protection of the city's inhabitants and the exclusion of those who have no part in it. Judgment and mercy live together there.

Verses 12–14. The city has twelve gates, inscribed with the names of Israel's twelve tribes, and twelve foundations (in a row, not on top of each other), engraven with the names of the twelve apostles. This sets forth the unity of the old and new Israel and hints that entrance to the city of God is through giving heed to the revelation of God made known to his people through the ages.

As the twelve tribes relate to Israel and its completeness, so the twelve apostles represent the whole apostolate. We need not ask whether Judas is out and Paul is in! The importance of the apostolate is its function as bearer of the "testimony of Jesus."

Verse 16. The city is four-square—a cube. Some remind us that the Greeks regarded the square as a symbol for perfection. It is more to the point to remember that the holy of holies was a cube. The entire city of God is a sanctuary, partaking of God's holiness. Hence there is no need for a temple—it is all temple.

The height of twelve thousand furlongs is fantastic—fifteen hundred miles! But it should not be so translated. The figure represents an infinite multiple of twelve. The meaning of this immense measurement is illustrated by the rabbinical saying that Jerusalem would be enlarged till it reached the gates of Damascus and exalted till it reached the throne of God. The city of God stretches from earth to heaven and unites them into one.

Verses 19-21. It is common in Jewish representations of the new Jerusalem to speak of its decoration by precious stones. But John's list of jewels on the foundation stones is not casual. First it appears to be identical with the jewels of the high priest's breastplate. Secondly it has been established from Philo, Josephus, and others that each of these jewels represented one of the twelve signs of the Zodiac. The extraordinary fact has come to light that the order of John's enumerating represents the path of the sun through the twelve signs, but in reverse order. This cannot be accidental. Charles deduces that John by this shows that the city of God and the Lamb has nothing to do with heathen speculations about the heavenly city of the gods.[2] In this I believe that he is right. The distinctiveness of the city is emphasized by the mention of the names of the twelve tribes of Israel on the gates and of the twelve apostles on the foundations. The city is founded on the apostolic testimony of Jesus. This is John's unique way of representing the truth that there is no other name under heaven given among men whereby we must be saved.

Verses 22:1 f. The city receives the sustenance of Christ. The river of water of life runs through it and the tree of life yields its fruits every month. These are to be interpreted spiritually. Through the church men will quench their spiritual thirst and hunger and gain healing for the wounds of sin.

Verse 22:3. The curse that has rested on the entire history of man at last has its antidote. Its effects have been completely overcome in the eternal city.

Verses 22:4 f. The goal of humanity is reached: man knows the vision of God, unity with him, and end of all darkness and fellowship in his eternal service.

Conclusion: The Meaning of Christ's Victory for Our Faith
1. Its Significance for the Christian Message

The French pastor Theo Preiss asked theologians to come down to earth and use plain language when talking about the Christian hope for man and his history. He set an excellent example in a striking statement which has since become famous: "We have dropped a good part of the biblical hope; others have picked it up, and now we receive it as a slap in our faces from the hands of the Marxist." [3] That dictum should be compared with one made by Christopher Hollis in a talk given on the BBC in England: "It will be a waste of time overthrowing Bolshevism unless it is overthrown by a trained theologian." [4] The idea of a theologian overthrowing Bolshevism is so remote from reality as to be humorous, but the link between these two statements is an important one which demands to be taken with utmost seriousness. It is the conviction that the inspiration of Marxism is the biblical hope drained of God.

I was fortunate to light on a book many years ago by Fritz Gerlich bearing the significant title *Der Kommunismus als Lehre vom tausendjährigen Reich (Communism as the Teaching of the Thousand Years Kingdom).* When this work appeared in 1920, its thesis was met with no little skepticism. Gerlich laboured to demonstrate that the genealogy of Marxism can be traced back from Marx the Jew, through the philosophers Hegel and Lessing, to the renowned German expositor of the Bible, Bengel. Marx's debt to Hegel is well known. Hegel and others were influenced by Lessing who believed that history is divided into three periods: its childhood, youth, and manhood corresponding to the Old Testament period, the New Testament period, and the emerging fulfilment now impending. For the origin of this teaching in Lessing, Gerlich maintained, we need look no further than the philosopher Crucius, who was a disciple of Bengel and who accepted the millennial instruction of his master.

Whether that pedigree is correct in all its details is not important. The main contention that the Marxist view of history is a secularized version of the teaching of the Bible is now widely acknowledged. Some of the early Communists did not hesitate to adapt the concepts of the Bible to their teaching. Consider for example the following statement from Wilhelm Weitling, whose writings were eagerly read by the French populace before Marx became a Communist:

A new Messiah do I see coming with the sword, to realise the teaching of the first. He will be placed through his courage at the head of the revolutionary army, and with it will bring to ruins the rotten structure of the old social order. He will lead the flood of tears into the sea of forgetfulness and change the earth into a paradise. . . . You poor, deceived but good natured people! Sleep on, till the trumpets and alarm call you to the last judgment. Then sweep away the men of Wittenburg and Rome (= Protestants and Catholics!), who preach about thrones and sacks of gold to mock your nakedness. Then will unity lift up the standard of neighborly love in your countries, your young men will fly with it to the ends of the earth, and the world will be transformed into a garden and mankind into a family.[5]

Here is a deliberate transformation of biblical teaching into a revolutionary eschatology. And this kind of procedure is not a thing of the past only. In the forecourt of the Moscow art gallery there stands today a statue of a workman beating a broad sword with a hammer. The bottom of the sword is assuming the shape of a plowshare, and an inscription on the base of the statue reads, "We must bend our swords into plowshares." It is doubtful that many Russians realize that this sentence is a conscious echo of words found in the books of Isaiah and Micah; but the sculptor will have known it, and he intended more than the noble ideal of his statue. The Old Testament prophets declared that men will beat their swords into plowshares and their spears into pruning hooks in the time when God establishes his kingdom among men. The Marxist rejects the God reference and affirms that *his* hands will achieve this by their own strength.

This is the secular hope that dominates the largest segment of Europe; it has taken over the largest nation in the world (China) and it has the prospect of taking over multitudes more. What has the church to say to it?

The church could say everything that needs to be said. In reality it has nothing to say. For fifteen hundred years any form of hope in an earthly kingdom of Christ has been viewed by the churches with something akin to horror. Largely owing to the immense influence of Augustine on the one hand and the espousal of millennarianism by the sects on the other, Catholics and Protestants have united in rejecting it. When asked what alternative hope they have for man in this world the official answer is: None at all. The world will be destroyed at the advent of Christ to give place to an eternal heaven and hell in which history will be forgotten. Since, however, immortality has now become a tenuous proposition to many and the doctrine of resurrection virtually abandoned, this prospect is so empty of reality to multitudes of Christians it can be said without contradiction that on the whole the Christian church is powerless to confront the Marxist on the issue of hope for mankind. The church has lost its message of hope. The Marxists have taken it up from them, adapted it to their own philosophy, dressed it up in their economic jargon, and then preached it as the only hope for the world.

What then is the church to do in face of this situation? The answer is surely clear: if the church has dropped its hope, it must pick it up again. That will mean that it must take the book of Revelation seriously once more, and recognize that it is a Christian book with authentic Christian doctrine. A curious situation exists with regard to the book of Revelation. Almost all modern scholars consider that this book teaches an earthly realization of the triumphant kingdom of Christ at his glorious advent. Almost all of them reject it as an integral part of the Christian hope. Why? Because it is, as they say, "Jewish." The belief that there will be a preliminary manifestation of the triumphant kingdom of God on earth is to be found in various forms in certain Jewish apocalyptic writings outside the Bible, and it became the object of much speculation by Jewish rabbis. This is hardly adequate ground for rejecting the teaching of a Christian book. These Jewish writings to which reference is made, and the Jewish teachers who speculated on the kingdom of the Messiah, also teach that God is one and holy; that there will be a resurrection of the dead, a last judgment and a new creation; and they call for men to trust God and be found in holiness at the last day. We do not reject *these* things because they were taught by devout Jews. In any case the book of Revelation is not "Jewish" in the sense of being sub-Christian. Its center is the crucified and risen Lord, and from first to last the book is testimony to him.

It is generally recognized that a major influence for the millennial doctrine of the book of Revelation was not in fact writings outside the Bible, but the book of Ezekiel, chapters 38—39; 40—48. But there may have been influences more decisive for John than Ezekiel and Jewish writers contemporary with him, namely early Christian teaching. Apart from the apostolic tradition of doctrine, it is quite certain that John would have known and used the prayer which Jesus taught his disciples to pray. The burden of that prayer is:

> Thy kingdom come,
> Thy will be done,
> On earth as in heaven.

There are many scholars who are prepared to maintain that the *teaching* of Jesus about the kingdom coincides with the implications of this prayer for the kingdom. Jesus certainly does not teach a doctrine of the millennium, but he does teach the coming of the kingdom of God among men through his own redemptive ministry. And there are indications in his teaching that he looked for the triumph of that kingdom in this world—as the prayer he taught suggests.

Moreover it is the acknowledged heart of Christian

doctrine that in the work of Christ the turn of the ages took place. From Easter onwards the history of this world stands under the dominance of a resurrection life, that of the risen Lord. The New Testament letters make it plain that the great unveiling at the end of the age will show who is the Lord of *this* age and that it will initiate a further era of his sovereignty (see 1 Cor. 15:20–28; Phil. 2:9–11). Accordingly *the kingdom of Christ is present among men in this world now.* Every line in the New Testament is written in the consciousness of the truth of that affirmation. The book of Revelation teaches that Christ's coming will bring that kingdom which is among men in this world now to decisive expression among men in this world then. There is no possibility of describing this as non-Christian or sub-Christian doctrine, let alone Jewish or humanist teaching. It is, to use jargon familiar to theologians, Christological eschatology, and it develops the implications of the doctrine of Christ the risen Redeemer.

It was reasoning of this kind which led Visser 't Hooft, former secretary of the World Council of Churches, to declare, "Because he reigns already we may and must see the world and all that is in it as the theatre in which that glory is to be manifested." [6] It led J. E. Fison, now bishop of Salisbury in England, to a similar viewpoint, couched in language which closely links with the train of thought with which we began:

Only if we believe in victory here can we meet the Marxist challenge on its own battlefield, and having defeated it there move on to the triumphs beyond of which it has no inkling. To this hope of God's triumph on earth we are committed if our hope is genuinely Christian.[7]

The verdict of the greatest commentator on the book of Revelation is worthy of note here. R. H. Charles, wrote:

The object of the Seer is to proclaim the coming of God's kingdom on earth, and to assure the Christian Church of the final triumph of goodness, not only in the individual or within its own borders, not only throughout the kingdoms of the world and in their relations one to another, but also throughout the whole universe. Thus its gospel was from the beginning at once individualistic and corporate, national and international and cosmic. . . . Gifted with an insight that the pessimist wholly lacks, he (John) can recognise the full horror of the evils that are threatening to engulf the world, and yet he never yields to one despairing thought of the ultimate victory of God's cause on earth. He greets each fresh conquest achieved by triumphant wrong with a fresh trumpet call to greater faithfulness, even when that faithfulness is called to make the supreme sacrifice . . . So with song and thanksgiving he marks each stage of the world strife which is carried on ceaselessly and inexorably till, as in 1 Corinthians 15:24–27, every evil power in heaven or earth, or under the earth, is overthrown and destroyed for ever.[8]

2. Its Significance for the Church's Life

There is one striking difference between the church since the Constantine era and the church in the apostolic age. The church is now a community which tends to be determined by the past—by its traditions and the history that gave it birth. For this reason it is always in danger of living in the past and failing to be an instrument of God's power in the present.

In the New Testament the church is a community dominated by the reality of the kingdom of God. It lives in the shadow of an accomplished redemption, it anticipates an event in the future which will form the counterpart and completion of that redemption, and it is sustained in the time between by the Spirit of the Lord who has come and is to come. Otherwise expressed, the church has been brought into being by the coming of the kingdom of Christ, it presses forward to the victory of Christ's kingdom, and it lives by participation in the first and in anticipation of the second.

While the first ardor of hope settled down with the passing of the years, this remained the essential outlook of the church until the time when it exchanged hope for the world for a settlement with the powers of this world. Since that time (the Constantinian era) the doctrine of the coming of Christ and his kingdom has tended to be a dogma without power. The doctrine will recover its power when the church freshly grasps the centrality of Christ in world history, the sufficiency of his redemption for all mankind, and the breadth of his purpose for all times.

What the victory of Christ at his coming will mean for the church in relation to the world (in distinction from the church in relation to Christ) is hinted at but not described in John's book. "They shall be priests of God and of Christ, and shall reign with him for a thousand years," writes John (Rev. 20:6). Priestly ministry suggests reference to the world in relation to God in Christ. The church will be in a measure not known before an advocate for the Lord, even as it will, in a measure not known before, reign with Christ. Here is a prospect which attracts and eludes us in the measure that the church's resurrection fascinates and eludes our thought. G. B. Caird suggests that John viewed this in the light of Christ's own resurrection and activity in the world so that for Christians as for Christ resurrection means that they have been "let loose in the world." [9] The day will declare it, as it will a good many other things!

3. Its Significance for the Believer

The chief effect of this teaching on Christians is its provision of the context in which our life and work are set. It places us between two great victories, the resurrection of Christ to be Lord of the universe and the return of Christ to manifest his kingdom in power. This has a number of corollaries.

The Christian life is determined from first to last by the Lord of life. It begins and it ends in resurrection from the dead. The sting of death has forever been drawn for the Christian. His Lord is its conqueror.

The Christian life is dependent from first to last on the power of the risen Lord. "Because I live, you shall live also," said Jesus with his resurrection in view. His resurrection was the result of the divine action in him and on him. Our resurrection will be the result of that same divine action in us and on us. The word that brought creation into being is the word that gives life from the dead. The Christian hope therefore is not in his human nature as hopefully immortal but in the promise and power of Christ the Redeemer.

The Christian life is characterized from first to last by faith in the Lord of life and power. The model of faith in the New Testament is Abraham, the man who believed in the God who makes the dead to live, and so he believed that God could make his own (virtually) dead body produce a son. So too the Christian believes in the God who makes the dead to live in and through Christ. He experiences this when by faith he becomes one with Christ and begins to live by his resurrection life. He is to know this even more drastically at the end of the age when God raises him in the likeness of Christ. Any participation in the victory of Christ here and now is on the same terms: dependence on grace and yielding to it in faith. He who will give us victory in the end can give us grace to live in the next ten minutes and to the end of our days, and beyond.

With the poet therefore we cheerfully confess:

> Yea thro' life, death, thro' sorrow and thro' sinning,
>   He shall suffice me, for he hath sufficed:
> Christ is the end, for Christ was the beginning,
>   Christ the beginning, for the end is Christ.
>   F. W. H. Myers

Notes

Scripture quotations are from *The New English Bible* unless otherwise indicated. © The Delegates of the Oxford University Press, and the Syndics of the Cambridge University Press, 1970.

CHAPTER 3
[1] Martin Kiddle, *The Revelation of St. John* "The Moffatt New Testament Commentary," (New York and London: Harper and Brothers Publishers, 1940), p. 67.
[2] Theodore Zahn, *Zommentar zum NT.*
[3] Emil Brunner, *Eternal Life*, p. 200 f.
[4] Matthias Rissi, *Time and History: A Study on the Revelation*, Tr. G. C. Winsor (Richmond: John Knox Press, 1966), p. 104.

CHAPTER 4
[1] Emil Brunner, *Eternal Hope*, Tr. Harold Knight (London: Lutterworth Press, 1954), p. 80–81.
[2] Paul Althaus, *Die letzten Dinge*, p. 286.
[3] H. B. Swete, *The Apocalypse of St. John* (London: Macmillan and Co., Ltd., 1908), p. clx.
[4] Martin Buber, *Mamre, Essays in Religion*, Tr. Greta Hort (Westport: Greenwood Press, 1946), p. 30.

CHAPTER 5
[1] R. H. Charles, *The Revelation of St. John* "The International Critical Commentary," (Edinburgh: T. & T. Clark, 1920).
[2] *Op. cit.*
[3] Theo Preiss, *Life in Christ* (Naperville, Ill.: Alec R. Allenson, Inc., 1954), p. 62.
[4] *The Listener*, January, 1948, p. 131.
[5] The citation is from Weitling's book, *Die Menschheit wie sie ist und wie sie sein sollte* (i.e., Mankind as it is and as it ought to be),

published in Paris in 1838. The work is not available to me but is quoted in extenso by Gerlich, pp. 207 f.

[6] W. A. Visser 't Hooft, *The Kingship of Christ*, p. 95.

[7] George B. Caird, et. al., *The Christian Hope* (Naperville, Ill.: Alec R. Allenson, Inc., 1970), p. 213.

[8] Charles, *op. cit.*, Vol. I, pp. ciii–iv.

[9] G. B. Caird, *A Commentary on the Revelation of St. John the Divine*, "Black's New Testament Commentaries" (London: Adam & Charles Black, Ltd., 1966).